The Lingo Dictionary

of favourite Australian words and phrases

John Miller

Introduction

The Australian language or 'lingo' is a distinct and unique 'creature', one that has evolved from a mixing pot of cultures over the past 220 years and one that is continuing to evolve today. People from all backgrounds and nationalities have contributed to the lingo: Aboriginal, English, Irish, Scottish, Welsh, Chinese, other Asians, eastern European, Mediterraneans, New Zealanders, Pacific Islanders and Americans. Without this cultural mix we would not have the unique way of speaking the English language that helps make our lingo so interesting, and in many instances amusing.

The spoken form of Australian English, or Strine — where words are uttered with the mouth barely open and much use of the nasal passages to create a drawl (perhaps to keep out the flies) — is very distinctive, especially when combined with the jargon, slang and colloquialisms used widely. There is the jargon associated with different occupations and activities, the slang of different age groups and different communities and the expressions that find favour with today's fashions and trends. Accents vary slightly from state to state and sometimes even from region to region, and there are quite a few terms and expressions that are unique to states, regions and even population centres.

Aussies have a penchant for shortening words or names and then adding an 'ie', 'o' or 'y', such as in 'brekkie' for breakfast, 'muso' for musician and 'smithy' for a blacksmith. Also 'a' generally sounds more like an 'i' to those from other nations and thus tailor sounds more like 'tiler'. Our 'i' often comes out as 'oye' and thus a roof tiler sounds more like a 'toyler'.

Most words with a 't' or a double 't' are often pronounced with a 'd' sound, such as in 'liddle' for little. Another idiosyncrasy is that Australians don't often emphasise 'er' at the end of words with the resulting sound being more like 'ah', such as in 'bee-ah' instead of beer and 'weath-ah' rather than weather.

The letter 'h' is often pronounced as 'haitch' with the emphasis on the aspirant 'h', but when this letter appears at the beginning of a word the 'h' is often dropped altogether, such as in 'ere' for 'here'. Dropping the 'g' at the end of 'ing' words is also very common, such as in 'doin'.

Aussies also have a penchant for dropping letters to shorten words and thus government becomes 'gumment'. Other words are lengthened, such as new which often become 'knee-yew', picture becomes 'pic-a-cha' and nuclear becomes 'knee-yew-cle-ah'. There is also a habit of dropping the 'l' after a vowel, such as in 'Uh-stray-ee-ah' for Australia.

There are many terms associated with the rugged Aussie character which has been moulded by years of coping with a tough climate and even tougher conditions. Thus there is emphasis on robust, crude and at times disgusting slang terms and sayings but it is part of the Australian psyche and, therefore, impossible to leave out of any material written about the language. As such some of the terms and expressions included in this book may offend some people. There are also quite a few terms no longer in common use and, of course, many new words introduced owing to new influences on the Australian culture.

The Aussie lingo of today began on the ships of the First Fleet when a mix of convicts, settlers, soldiers and sailors spoke a variety of differing dialects and versions of British working-class slang. Among the words that would have made the trip to Australia and are now commonly used are 'bloke', 'booze', 'conk' and 'bloody'. When the convicts arrived on these shores many continued their habits from their former home and among the words they used are 'bludger', 'cove', 'nark', 'beak' and 'dunny'. In Britain at the time there were many regional dialects and these too made their way to Australia, each bringing their own words, phrases and expressions with examples including 'fair dinkum', 'chook', 'dag', 'billy', 'larrikin', 'burl' and 'fossick'. Australia also saw many Irish immigrants who brought with them words like 'barrack', 'gob', 'shenanigans' and 'youse'.

At the time of European settlement of Australia, the traditional owners of the land spoke more than 300 separate languages, many of which are now extinct. The Aussie lingo has borrowed many words from the Aboriginal languages, including 'budgerigar', 'dingo', 'kangaroo', 'koala', 'bindi-eye', 'yabby', 'boomerang', 'billabong', 'humpy', 'dilly', 'gibber', 'bung', 'cooee', 'yakka' and 'yabber'.

As Australian English continued to develop its own path, new local slang terms were coined and there are many of them, including 'battler', 'bonzer', 'bottler', 'chunder', 'digger', 'drongo', 'footy', 'G'day', 'hoon', 'norks', 'ocker', 'perv', 'sanger', 'sheila' and 'wowser'. There are also many slang phrases, many of which indicate the robust nature of Australia and our love of humour, including 'happy little vegemite', 'map of Tassie', 'like a shag on a rock', 'dry as a dead dingo's donger' and 'not much chop'.

I find the use of rhyming slang particularly clever and amusing. Rhyming slang first appeared among the cockneys of London's East End and while there is some cockney rhyming slang still used in Australia, the vast majority of this form of language had its origins right here, probably due to our love of humour and satire. Cockney versions still used include 'plates of meat' for 'feet' and 'elephant's trunk' for 'drunk'. Home-grown versions include 'bag of fruit' for 'suit', 'billy lid' for 'kid', 'Captain Cook' for 'look', 'Reg Grundies' for 'undies', 'Joe Blake' for 'snake', 'horse's hoof' for 'poof' and 'Noah's ark' for 'shark'. Often the rhyming word is dropped such as in 'Noah' for 'shark', 'Joe' for 'snake' and 'Jack', short for 'jack in the box', rhyming slang for 'pox'.

Just as there are in Britain, there are many regionalisms that only exist in certain states or regions of Australia. These are often based on geographical features or regional cultural differences. There are many examples, including those used to describe city-based four-wheel-drive vehicles that are seldom, or never, used in terrain that necessitates engaging the vehicles in four-wheel-drive, such as a 'Toorak tractor' or 'Toorak taxi' in Melbourne, a 'Dalkeith tractor' in Perth, 'Burnside warrior' in Adelaide, 'Kenmore tractor' in Brisbane, and in Sydney a 'Double Bay tractor', 'Balmain bulldozer', 'Balmoral bulldozer', 'Mosman tractor', 'North Shore tank' and 'Turramurra tractor'.

Although there are also overseas influences on our language, new slang is being invented every day by Australians to reflect new technology and shifts in cultural emphasis. Among the newcomers helping to further develop the unique Aussie lingo are 'doof', 'feral', 'filth', 'pov' and 'bowlo'. It is also interesting to note that a number of great Aussie expressions have also made their way overseas and even into the United States where 'crikey', 'no worries', 'onya' and 'fair dinkum', among others, are becoming more widely used.

There are also words and phrases in Australia that have died out as the generations have come and gone and as technology has advanced. These include many of the military terms that came into existence during World Wars I and II when many Australians were involved with wartime operations. Terms relating to cigarette usage are also slowly dying out as anti-smoking measures are increased while a number of terms used to describe pre-decimal currency have not survived the transformation.

If you are concerned about the loss of any of these expressions, just start using them again and they may be reinvented.

A

ABC An Australian-born Chinese or a derogatory term for a white Australian, stands for Aboriginal Bum Cleaner.

Abo A racist term for an Aboriginal.

Aboriginal suitcase or **briefcase** A racist term for a cask of wine.

Acca Dacca A nickname for the kings of Aussie rock AC/DC.

AC/DC Used to describe someone considered to be bisexual.

ace Someone or something that is excellent, outstanding or terrific.

ace it up To make something very good.

acid Another name for the drug LSD. Also if you **put the acid on** someone you are trying to pressure them to do something they many not want to do.

acre Slang for the backside or bottom and so called because it is an expanse, e.g. 'He was six axe handles across the acre'.

act the goat To behave foolishly or do something silly.

Adam, since Adam was a boy or a **pup** Refers to something that happened a long time ago or something that covers an extensive time, e.g. 'He's been doing it that way since Adam was a boy'.

Adelaide Used by people in eastern states to describe someone who is a little slow; Adelaide is half an hour behind the eastern states.

aerial ping pong A derogatory term used by followers of the rugby codes to describe Australian Rules football.

affluence of inkahol Another way of saying someone is under the influence of alcohol. It describes the effects of alcohol on speech.

after-grog bog or **AGB** A particularly noisy or smelly excrement produced after a big drinking session — often the next morning. Also called the post grog bog (PGB).

aggie 1. A playing marble. 2. Another name for a student studying agriculture.

aggro A shortened expression used to describe aggression or aggravation. If someone is using threatening behaviour it is often said they are 'being aggro'.

agricultural shot A wild or ill-considered shot in cricket so called as it is the sort of shot a farmer might make.

to get **air** In skating, surfing, basketball and the like the amount of height gained when getting airborne.

air head An empty headed, brainless person.

airs Abbreviation of the phrase 'airs and graces', meaning to be a little pretentious.

airy fairy Something of very little substance.

Albany doctor In the wheat belt of south-west WA this is the name given to a southerly sea breeze that blows after a hot day.

Al Capone Aussie rhyming slang for the telephone. Also 'Eau de Cologne'.

alko or **alkie** Abbreviation for alcoholic, a heavy drinker.

all alone like a country dunny On your own, by yourself.

all behind like Barney's bull Having a fat or large backside.

all ears Listening attentively to what's going on.

all over bar the shouting Something that is for all intents and purposes finished with.

all over it like a seagull on a sick prawn A crowd or throng gathered around something or someone.

all over the place like a mad woman's breakfast, **all over the shop** or **all over the place like a wet dog on lino** In complete confusion and disarray, not knowing whether you are coming or going.

all piss and wind All talk but no action, insincere.

all prick and ribs A description of someone who is skinny.

also-ran An unplaced horse in a race. Also used to describe a dud or a non-entity.

always in the shit Someone who is always in trouble.

amber fluid, **amber liquid** or **amber nectar** Colloquialisms for beer. Rather than say the word itself many drinkers use other words such as turps, drinks or suds. Others drop the word completely, simply saying 'have a few' or 'sink a few'.

ambo Slang for an ambulance officer or driver.

American screwdriver A hammer.

ammo Abbreviation of ammunition.

anal Obsessively self-controlled in relation to personality traits, such as neatness or stubbornness.

anal floss G-strings or items of underwear that ride up the bottom cleft. Also called **bum floss.**

anally retentive One who is meticulous and rigid about minor details.

anchors The brakes of a vehicle, e.g. 'Hit the anchors'.

angel gear The neutral gear of a vehicle when used in the practice of coasting. So called because of the likelihood of this practice leading to the driver becoming an angel.

animal A vulgar, brutish or disgusting person.

ankle A crass term for someone you don't like; it refers to the ankle being three feet lower than the sexual organs.

ankle biters Small children. A term made popular by entertainer Barry Humphries. Also called **rug rats**.

ano Abbreviation of anorexic.

anothery Slang for another drink of beer.

Anzac An abbreviation of Australian and New Zealand Army Corps, originally coined to describe soldiers from both countries who served in World War I. Since then the term has been widened to include all soldiers who have given their lives for their country. It is also used to describe typical Australian men seen to have the same courage and determination as shown by the Anzacs at Gallipoli.

Anzac biscuits Biscuits for which the main ingredients are rolled oats and golden syrup. A recipe for Anzac cakes was published in 1915 and six years later a recipe for Anzac crispies united the ingredients and method. By 1927 they had become known as Anzac biscuits.

Anzac Day A public holiday in Australia and New Zealand on 25 April marking the anniversary of the landing of the Australian and New Zealand Army Corps at Gallipoli in 1915. Soldiers from both countries marked the day with memorial services in 1916 and two years later the same idea surfaced in Sydney. It has since become a day for Australians and New Zealanders around the world to remember those who have made the supreme sacrifice for their country in any theatre of war.

ape 1. A large, uncouth, boorish person. 2. G**o ape over**, or **go apeshit** To go crazy or mad about something.

ape hangers The handlebars of a motorbike or bike that rise above the level of the rider's shoulder.

Apple Isle Another name for Tasmania, famed for its apple orchards.

apples Commonly used in the phrase 'She'll be apples' meaning all is well or will work out well.

apples and pears Rhyming slang for stairs.

apple sauce Rhyming slang for horse.

apricots Another term for testicles.

aqua bog An excrement done while swimming in the ocean.

arc up To become upset, get one's back up or become angry.

argue the toss To dispute a decision or a command.

argy-bargy An argument, e.g. 'the two were engaged in some argy-bargy'.

aristotle Rhyming slang for a bottle, usually full of beer.

Arizona strawberries Slang term for baked beans, so named because Arizona is dry and the strawberries would not be very big in this climate. Believed to be a term only used in Australia.

arse 1. A slang term for the buttocks or anus. Also used to describe a contemptible person and used in many offensive phrases. 2. **Shift your arse** or **Get your arse into gear** Terms used to get people or animals to hurry up or get active. 3. **Not know your arse from your elbow** Describes someone who knows very little. 4. **arsehole** or **arse wipe** A contemptible person or someone who has offended you. 5. **arse licker** or **up his arse** Someone who flatters or obediently carries out the orders of a superior in order to gain favour. 6. **arsy** or **what arse** Someone who is lucky or fortunate. 7. **arse about** Something that is back to front. 8. **arse over tit** To fall heavily. 9. **up your arse** A term used towards someone who has made you upset or angry, e.g. 'You can stick the job up your arse'. 10. **arse drops out of** something Describes something that has failed dismally. 11. **get the arse** or **arseholed** Dismissal from work or rejection, e.g. 'She's given me the arse' or 'I got arseholed'. 12. **arse end** The tail end or the base of something. 13. **arse end of the world** A hideous or terrible place. 14. **arse up** Incorrect or wrong side up.

arty Describes anyone who is interested in or practises any form of the arts.

arty farty A derogatory term for someone involved with or practising in the arts.

arvo An Australian pronunciation of the first two syllables of the word afternoon and used to describe that part of the day. **S'arvo** is often used for 'this afternoon'.

as dry as a bark hut To be very thirsty.

as much hope as the *Titanic* with Mark Latham in the wheelhouse To have very little or no hope. Mark Latham is a former unsuccessful ALP leader.

as the crow flies In a direct route from one place to another.

as thick as two planks Someone who is not very intelligent.

Athens of the south Generally used to refer to Melbourne, which has the second-largest Greek population of any city in the world, after Athens. Also used to refer to Adelaide because of its sunny climate.

at it 1. Engaged in sexual intercourse. 2. Having an argument.

aunty or **auntie** Apart from being used as an affectionate version of the formal aunt it is also used by many Australians as a description of the Australian Broadcasting Corporation (the ABC) in reference to its image as a kindly and well-intentioned, if old-fashioned, guardian of standards.

Aussie Someone or something that is Australian

Aussie battler A member of the Australian working class who has to struggle to make a living. Also known as the **little Aussie battler**.

Aussie salute or **Australian salute** The constant practice of brushing away flies from your face with your hand and arm. Also called the **Barcoo salute.**

average Typical Australian understatement that doesn't mean average at all, it actually means pretty bad, e.g. 'I'm feeling pretty average after last night'.

away with the fairies or **off with the fairies** Describes either someone who is living in a state of fantasy or projects that don't appear to be based on reality. Sometimes **pixies** is used instead of fairies.

awning over the toy shop A beer belly on a male.

axe To be dismissed from work, as in 'She got the axe'.

axe handle A rough unit of measurement, e.g. 'He is a big bloke … about ten axe handles wide', meaning he is broad-shouldered.

ay or **eh** A common expression used by many Australians to inquire about something, to seek clarification for something not understood or asking someone to repeat what they have just said. Also a syllable that many Queenslanders add to the end of phrases, sentences or statements, e.g. 'I went to the footy, ay' or 'Let's have a beer, ay'.

B

b A euphemism for bastard, especially when the word was taboo, e.g. 'That bloke was a right b'.

babe 1. A familiar way of addressing a woman, e.g. 'Hey babe, how ya going?' 2. An attractive female, e.g. 'She's a real babe'. This was considered sexist but in more recent times has become increasingly used by both sexes with some women now using the term to refer to an attractive male.

babe alert A statement alerting others of the opportunity to look at an attractive member or group of the opposite sex.

babefest An event at which there are many attractive females or males.

baby-poo brown or **baby-cack brown** A displeasing brown colour, reminiscent of a baby's faeces.

backblocks Anywhere that is a long way from the city, distant from mainstream or urban living. Can be considered to be the country or even the outer suburbs of bigger cities.

backchat To answer back in an impertinent manner.

backhander A bribe or illicit financial transaction. Also an unofficial so-called bonus provided for carrying out a project.

back o' beyond As far out in the bush or the outback as one could get.

back of Bourke In the middle of nowhere. Bourke is a town in the north-west of NSW generally considered to be in the outback.

backs to the wall A catchphrase used by homophobic men to warn that a gay man is in the vicinity.

bad An ironic reversal of meaning for good and primarily used by young people.

bad hair day A day when you cannot get your hair to look good or to look as you would like it to. Also refers to a bad day in general.

badmouth To speak unfavourably of someone.

bad trot A run of bad luck or misfortune.

baffle with bullshit To deceive someone with big words, difficult concepts or lies.

bag or **old bag** 1. A derogatory description of a woman. 2. A good haul of wickets obtained by a bowler in cricket. 3. A bookmaker's satchel into which the bookie puts his money. 4. **bagging, to give someone a** To criticise someone or something, to knock someone or to put them down. 5. Another word for the breathalyser, e.g. 'to blow in the bag'.

baggy green A slang term for the Australian Test cricket cap.

bag o' fruit Rhyming slang for a man's suit.

bag of tricks A term used to describe a tradesman's tool box or a collection of things.

bags or **bagsed** A cry used to stake a claim before someone else and commonly used by kids, e.g. 'I bagsed it first'.

bail or **bail out** 1. To leave something or to depart. 2. To leave in a cowardly manner.

bald as a badger or **bald as a bandicoot** Someone who is totally bald.

Bali belly Diarrhoea or a stomach illness, as often suffered by travellers to Bali or South-East Asia.

ball A testicle.

ball and chain Used in a jocular way as another term for wife.

ballistic To explode with anger, e.g. 'He really went ballistic'.

balls 1. The testicles. To **have someone by the balls** is to have them in your power. When something **stands out like dogs balls** it means that something is very obvious. 2. Courage or moral strength, e.g. 'He's got the balls to attempt that'.

balls 'n all To attempt something aggressively and enthusiastically.

balls up To make a mess of an attempt or to bungle, a blunder.

ball tearer 1. Something that is very good, e.g. 'This song is a real ball tearer'. 2. An aggressive woman.

Balmain kiss A headbutt. This is the Aussie equivalent to the British Liverpool kiss and came about because the now refined Sydney suburb of Balmain was once the home of wharfies and rough working-class men.

banana A slang term for a $50 note owing to its colour.

banana bender Anyone who hails from Queensland, where most of Australia's bananas are grown.

bananas Going crazy or mentally unstable, e.g. 'She's gone bananas'.

band moll A female groupie who sleeps with the men in a rock band.

B and S A bachelor and spinster ball, which is a dance held for young people in country areas.

bang 1. An act of sexual intercourse. A red-hot lover is said to **bang like a dunny door**. Also used to rate a person's sexual ability. 2. A way of intensifying a statement, e.g. 'He parked the car bang in the middle of the car park'.

banged up A phrase describing a female who is pregnant.

banger 1. A sausage. 2. A beat-up old car.

bang on or **bang on the knocker** To get something exactly right, dead centre, bull's eye.

banker A river full up to the top of its banks.

bar A call used by children indicating you are safe during a chasing game.

barbed wire Queensland slang for a Fourex beer. The 'XXXX' of the brand's name resembles barbed wire.

barbie A popular abbreviation for a barbecue, both the cooking apparatus and the social gathering. To be **a couple of bangers short of a barbie** or **one steak short of a barbie** means you are not very intelligent.

barf To vomit. A **barf bag** is a paper bag used for travel sickness.

bargain Terrific or excellent.

barge in To force one's way in.

barmy Crazy. If you are really crazy you may be called **barmy as a bandicoot**.

Barmy Army An Australian expression for English cricket supporters.

barney An argument or a fight, e.g. 'We had a big barney and she walked out'.

barra An abbreviation of the fish barramundi.

barrack 1, To make noisy and public comment, often about a sports match or a meeting. 2. To support a sports player or team, e.g. 'I barrack for the Wallabies'.

barrel To knock someone or something over by running into or striking hard.

Barrier Reef Rhyming slang for teeth.

barry 1. A terrible blunder, mistake or poor performance. Shortened form of **Barry Crocker**, which is rhyming slang for shocker. 2. An unpopular person without friends, same as **Neville** or **Nigel**.

base over apex Upside down or head over heels.

bash 1. An attempt or try, e.g. 'I'll give it a bash'. 2. A party or an active social occasion. 3. To criticise verbally. Among our favourite 'bashing' subjects are politicians, unions, social climbers, tall poppies, entrepreneurs or anyone who rises above the pack.

bash the spine Slang term for sleep.

basin cut A poor haircut that appears as though the barber placed an inverted basin or bowl on the head and trimmed the hair below the rim. Also **bowl cut**.

basket A euphemism for bastard.

basket case A person believed to be crazy or stressed so much that they cannot function properly.

bastard 1. Originally a person born of unmarried parents but the term is now used to describe an unpleasant or a disliked person. 2. So commonly used in Australia that it now often refers to anyone, and not always in a derogatory manner, e.g. 'You poor bastard'. 3. Anything that causes difficulty or aggravation, e.g. 'What a bastard of a day'.

bat An ugly woman.

bat and ball Rhyming slang for both wall and stall, e.g. 'I bat and balled the car'.

batch or **bach** An abbreviation of the word bachelor and used for men who are alone or who look after themselves while their wife or partner is away. It can also now be used to refer to a woman living out of home. Also **batching**.

bat for the other team From a heterosexual perspective, to be homosexual or vice versa.

bath dodger A slang term for an English person.

bat out of hell When someone is moving at great speed.

battleaxe A crabby, old, unfriendly person.

battler A decent and fair person who persists despite setbacks. Working-class Australians are also known as **little Aussie battlers**.

beak 1. A person's nose. 2. A judge.

beam The backside, e.g. 'He was pretty wide across the beam'.

bean counter Slang term for an accountant.

beanie brigade People who wear beanies and checked flannel shirts.

bean pole A tall, lanky person. Also known as **a long streak of pelican shit**.

beast A powerful machine of any type but primarily used to describe a great big car.

beating around the bush Not getting to the point of the subject.

beaut Good or excellent, e.g. 'That's beaut, mate'.

beauty, bewdi or **bewdi bottler** 1. An exclamation of excited approval or joy, e.g. 'You little beauty'. 2. Something of very good quality.

because it was there An ironic phrase used to explain why a challenge was carried out or a feat achieved. From a reply Edmund Hillary once gave when asked why he had climbed Mount Everest.

beef 1. Body weight, muscle or fat, e.g. 'He's got plenty of beef on him'. 2. A complaint or grumble.

beer coat The ability to endure cold weather gained from getting so drunk that you can barely feel anything.

beer gut A large, rounded stomach on a male from drinking beer.

beer map A map drawn in beer that has been spilt on the bar or table.

beer o'clock Time for a beer, generally after work but it could be anytime, depending on the individual's thirst.

beer wench A woman who gets the beers for a bunch of blokes. Also a term to describe barmaids.

bee's dick or **bee's whisker** A very small amount, e.g. 'I missed it by a bee's dick'.

bee's knees The best or the greatest.

bell A telephone call, e.g. 'I'll give you a bell later'.

belly flop, **belly buster** or **belly whacker** A dive in which your stomach hits the water first with a loud and painful slap.

bench warmer A reserve for a sporting team who does not get many games. Also now commonly used in non-sporting applications for someone who is waiting to play the main game.

bend the elbow The popular Australian pastime of drinking beer.

bent Corrupt.

berko To go berserk or to be angry in an unreasonable way.

berley 1. Any bait that is thrown into the water to attract fish. 2. The practice of throwing bait into the water to attract fish.

bestest A superlative of best, e.g. 'She's my bestest friend'.

betcha A shortened version of 'bet you'.

better half A slang term for one's husband, wife or partner.

better than a poke in the eye with a blunt stick A phrase used to describe doing something that is better than what you are doing at the time.

betting with rubber bands Betting with the last of your money after a day of losses, with the rubber bands referring to those that held the wad of money you started the day with.

best thing since sliced bread Something considered to be extremely worthwhile.

bevan A term for on uncultured, unrefined or loutish person, similar to bogan. More commonly used in Queensland.

bevan heaven A 7-Eleven convenience store.

bi Abbreviation of bisexual.

Bible basher A person of Christian faith who attempts to forcefully persuade you of their religious convictions.

bickie or **bikkie** 1. Commonly used term for a biscuit. 2. A dollar or money. If someone earns a lot of money they are said to earn **big bickies** or **big bucks**.

biddy A fussy old woman.

Bidgee An abbreviation of Murrumbidgee River.

bich A polite way of saying bitch.

biff or **biffo** Fighting or physically aggressive behaviour. To **go the biff** is to get into a fight.

big A To get the arse or the sack from work.

big ask A request that is difficult to fulfil.

big C Cancer.

big call A gutsy statement.

big day Your wedding day.

big fellow upstairs Used when referring to God.

biggie 1. Something large. 2. An adult, as opposed to a 'littlie' or child.

big girl's blouse An effeminate or sissy man.

big jobs A term for 'number twos', commonly used when addressing young children.

big note To boast about your own importance. A person who makes a habit of doing this is called a **big noter**.

big smoke The city or a built-up area as opposed to the countryside.

big spit To vomit.

big sticks The term used for the main goal posts in Aussie Rules. A goal through the big sticks is worth six points.

big time To a great extent, e.g. 'You owe me big time'.

big whoop A rhetorical expression meaning 'Who cares?', spoken in a sarcastic tone.

bike A derogatory term for a woman who sleeps around.

bikie A member of a gang of motorcycle riders.

billabong A waterhole or a lake formed by a river bend that has been cut off. Taken from the Wiradjuri Aboriginal language of central NSW.

billy 1. A tin can with a wire handle generally suspended over a campfire for the purpose of boiling water to make tea. To **boil the billy** is to have a break from work or a journey. To **swing the billy** originally meant to swing the can from a stick over a fire but has come to mean taking a billy full of tea and swinging it around in a circular motion at arm's length in order to settle the tea leaves. 2. A bong for smoking marijuana.

billy cart A small four-wheeled cart, often homemade and generally consisting of a box placed on a board and positioned over a fixed rear axle with the board extending to the movable front axle that is steered by a rope held by the driver in the box. Also called a **go-cart**, a **hill trolley** in WA or a **soap box** in WA and SA.

billy lid Rhyming slang for a kid or child.

billyo or **billy-oh** A non-existent place you tell somebody you don't like to go to. It was originally a euphemism for the devil or hell when used in certain phrases. To **run like billyo** is to run like the devil, to **go to billyo** is to go to hell and if it is **off to billyo** it is far away.

bingle A minor car accident, usually with damage to the vehicles only and not the occupants.

bird A derogatory word for a woman.

birdwatcher A male who looks at women a lot.

birthday suit Naked — a reference to what you were wearing when you were born.

bish or **bich** A more polite way of saying bitch.

bit Sexual intercourse, e.g. 'Fancy a bit?' A **bit on the side** refers to sexual intercourse outside of a partnership or marriage.

bitch 1. Used in a derogatory way to describe women, particularly those who are disagreeable or malicious. It has become more common as a term to describe any woman. 2. It can also be directed at men, although mostly in a joking way. Thus a guy who makes a nasty comment can be called a bitch. 3. A description of anything that annoys you. 4. To complain or gripe is to **bitch about** something.

bitch fight A fight between two women. Also called a **cat fight** or **scrag fight**.

bite To cadge off someone or to **put the bite on** them.

bite your bum A firm no or telling someone to bugger off.

a **bit more choke and you would have started** Said to someone who has just passed wind in a minor manner that sounds like a motor struggling to start.

a **bit of all right** An attractive person, e.g. 'She's a bit of all right'.

a **bit of how's your father** Sexual intercourse.

bit of skirt A woman seen as a sex object or as a bit of all right.

bite To borrow money or to ask someone for money, e.g. 'He put the bite on me'.

bitzer or **bitser** Abbreviation of 'bits of this and bits of that'. It is often used to describe a dog of mixed or unknown breed.

bizzo Another term for business in the most general sense.

black aspro A cola soft drink used to cure a hangover.

black budgie A blowfly.

black mariah A police van for the conveyance of people in custody.

black over Bill's mother An approaching thunderstorm.

black rat A can of Bundaberg Rum and cola.

black snake Slang term for a crowbar.

black stump Any part of Australia considered to be a long way away from civilisation. **Beyond the black stump** refers to a long distance. **This side of the black stump** refers to somewhere closer to civilisation. There are a number of places in Australia that claim to be the site of the original black stump, including Coolah and Merriwagga in NSW and Blackall in Queensland, while there is also one at Cowell in SA.

blazes A non-existent place to tell someone you don't like to go to, e.g. 'Go to blazes'.

bleeding dog's eye A meat pie with tomato sauce.

blimey An exclamation of surprise or amazement, sometimes lengthened to **blimey Charlie**.

blind Being drunk to the point of not being able to see properly.

blinder Incredibly amazing, e.g. 'She had a blinder of a game'.

blind Freddy could see that A phrase used to state that something is really obvious.

blind mullet Excrement floating in the water in which you are swimming. Also a **blind trout** or a **pollywaffle**, in reference to the chocolate snack bar which it resembles. In Sydney they go under the name of a **Bondi cigar** or **Bondi shark** and in Victoria a **Werribee trout** or **King River prawn**.

Blinky Bill Rhyming slang for a dill or stupid person.

blister 1. A parking infringement attached to a car window. 2. Aussie rhyming slang for sister.

blob 1. A fat person. 2. In cricket a score of nought or a duck.

block The head. Used in phrases like **lost your block** or **do your block**, which mean to lose your temper. To **knock your block off** is to punch or hit someone else in the head.

blockhead A slow person.

bloke 1. A slang word for a man, especially a down-to-earth man without pretensions. **A good bloke** is one of the highest accolades that can be bestowed on a man in Australia while **not a bad bloke** is not as high on the scale. 2. A boyfriend, e.g. 'I'd like you to meet my new bloke'. 3. An affectionate name for a male animal.

blokette A woman who can hold her own with the men.

blokey Masculine but in a crass way.

blonde Stupid or silly and taken from the image of a dumb blonde, e.g. 'She's having a blonde moment'.

bloodhouse A really rough pub.

blood nut A redhead.

blood's worth bottling A phrase used to describe an excellent person, e.g. 'His blood's worth bottling'.

bloody Formerly the quintessential Australian swear word, also known as the 'great Australian adjective', but now so prevalent that it is almost considered not to be a swear word at all. It is generally used to add emphasis as in 'bloody beauty' and can also be inserted into the middle of words such as 'abso-bloody-lutely'. It used to be considered taboo and never to be used in polite society, which gave rise to euphemisms such as **blooming**, **bleeding**, **blinking**, **flaming** and **ruddy**.

bloody oath Definitely right. Used by many as a form of emphasis.

bloody well Used to add emphasis or intensity to a statement, e.g. 'He bloody well does live there'.

blotting paper Food eaten when you are out on a drinking binge.

blotto Very drunk.

blow 1. To have a rest from work. 2. A big wind or a big storm. Also to **blow a blue dog off its chain**. 3. To brag or boast. 4. To abscond or flee, e.g. 'He's blown through'. 5. To ejaculate or experience orgasm. 6. To fail, e.g. 'I've really blown it'. 7. Cocaine. 8. A euphemism for damn, e.g. 'Blow that for a joke'. 9. A stroke of the handpiece by a shearer.

blower Another name for the telephone, e.g. 'Why don't you get on the blower?'

blowie A blowfly.

blow-in An uninvited person or an unexpected visit.

blow in the bag To undergo a breathalyser test.

blow it out your arse An exclamation of contempt to someone you are angry with.

blow me down An expression of amazement.

blow out 1. To amaze someone. 2. A lengthening of the odds in betting.

blow shit out of someone To reprimand someone severely.

blow through To leave or depart.

blow up To lose your temper.

blow your dough To waste your money.

bludge 1. A person who is lazy or doesn't work and who benefits from the efforts of others is said to be having a bludge and is called a **bludger**. 2. To cadge or borrow something, e.g. 'Can I bludge a ride?' 3. Something that is easy to do.

blue 1. A fight, dispute or row. 2. A mistake. 3. A nickname for someone with red hair, also **bluey**.

blue-arsed fly A term used for someone who is very busy, e.g. 'He's going like a blue-arsed fly'.

blue blazes A term used to intensify a statement, e.g. 'What in the blue blazes are you doing?'

blue flyer The adult female of the red kangaroo, noted for exceptional speed.

blue heeler 1. A purebred Australian dog with black or red face and ears, and dark blue body speckled with lighter blues. 2. A police officer.

blue movie A pornographic film.

blue murder In serious trouble.

blue swimmer A $10 note, the colour of which resembles a blue swimmer crab.

bluey 1. A rolled blanket, originally blue, containing the possessions of a traveller in the bush. To **hump the bluey** is to live the life of a swagman. 2. In Tasmania, a large grey-blue woollen coat or jacket. 3. Hospital slang for a blue plastic bedsheet for incontinent patients. 4. A summons issued for a traffic or parking offence. 5. A blue cattle dog. 6. A blue-tongue lizard, a blue swimmer crab or a blue yabby. 7. A $10 note.

blunder A mistake.

boardies Abbreviation of boardshorts.

boat race A relay competition between teams of drinkers to see which team can drink its beer fastest.

bob Slang term for a shilling, which became 10 cents after decimal currency was introduced in 1966. Also used to describe money in general, e.g. 'He's not short of a bob'.

bobby dazzler An excellent person or thing.

Bob Hope 1. Rhyming slang for dope. 2. Rhyming slang for soap.

Bob Hope's brother Used to describe someone or something that has no hope.

bod 1. A person. 2. A body.

bodgie or **bodgy** 1. False, worthless or of poor quality as in a 'bodgie repair job' or a 'bodgie movie'. 2. A young hooligan or lout from the 1950s and 1960s. 3. A large playing marble.

bodgie up To mock up or fake.

bog 1. Going to the toilet to do 'number twos'. 2. A slang word for the toilet, also **bog house** or **bogger**. 3. A putty-like material used for patching vehicle bodies.

bogan 1. An uncultured or loutish person, especially in WA and Tasmania. 2. A fool or an idiot, especially in NSW and Victoria.

bogan juice Iced coffee, as it is considered to be a drink that is primarily consumed by bogans.

bogey 1. A swim or bath in a creek or waterhole. 2. A piece of nasal mucus.

bog in To eat heartily, to tuck into a meal.

bog standard Not containing any special features, the standard model.

bogus 1. Very bad, no good or unfair. 2. Used by young people to mean the opposite, as in excellent, brilliant or terrific, e.g. 'That was absolutely bogus'.

boiler An uncomplimentary term for an older woman, also a **tough old bird**.

boilover A win by a long-priced entrant in a race or contest.

bollocky or **bollicky** A state of nakedness. If you are **in the bollocky** you are in the nude.

bolt To run away or to escape from custody.

bolt in To win easily.

bomb 1. An old car, particularly one that has been extensively used and not necessarily looked after. 2. A jump into the water with the knees tucked into the chest and the arms wrapped around the knees so as to make a big splash. 3. To fail a test or to do poorly. Also **bomb out**.

bombshell 1. A sexy woman. 2. A sudden, unexpected action, e.g. 'The decision was a real bombshell'.

Bondi chest The chest of a puny man, because 'Bondi is far from Manly'.

Bondi shark or **Bondi cigar** A floating piece of human excrement in the ocean.

Bondi tram A metaphor for a speedy departure. Used because the now defunct tram service to Bondi Beach from Sydney was notoriously fast, e.g. 'He shot through like a Bondi tram'.

bone 1. Having a gripe or specific problem with someone, e.g. 'I've got a bone to pick with you'. 2. If someone **points the bone** at someone they wish them bad luck. 3. An erect penis, also a **boner**.

bonecrusher A heavy tackle in a contact sport.

bonehead A stupid or obstinate person.

boneshaker 1. Any vehicle with bad, or hard, suspension. 2. An ancient and rickety bicycle.

bong An apparatus for smoking marijuana.

bonk 1. To have sexual intercourse. 2. To hit someone on the head but not too forcefully.

bonkable Attractive enough to have sexual intercourse with.

bonker A large marble.

bonkers Crazy, insane or out of control.

bonus Excellent or great.

bonzer or **bonza** Something that is very pleasing. A bonzer bloke is someone who can be trusted and is good to be around.

boob tube A strapless, tubular top worn by a woman and primarily covering the breasts.

boofhead An idiot or a stupid person.

boofy 1. A brawny man who is not very intelligent. 2. Hair having lots of volume. 3. Puffed out, e.g., 'The woman wore a boofy blouse'.

boogie or **booger** A piece of nasal mucus that has come out of the nose.

bookie Abbreviation of bookmaker.

boomer 1. A large male kangaroo. 2. Something impressive, a great success. 3. A large, crashing wave.

boomerang 1. A word from the Dharug Aboriginal language describing a traditional throwing stick, particularly one that returns. 2. A borrowed item that must be returned, e.g. 'You can borrow the book but it's a boomerang'.

boondocks or **boonies** Any remote region.

boot 1. A kick, e.g. 'I'll give you a boot up the backside'. Also to **put the boot in** is to attack unmercifully. 2. Rejection or ejection, e.g. 'I got the boot from work today'. 3. The trunk of a car.

boot home To ride home a winner, or to urge the horse to go faster.

bootlace Useless. If you are **not someone's bootlace** you are no good at doing what that person does.

bootlicker Someone who flatters, or crawls.

boots and all Slang for giving it everything, referring to strength or resources.

booze An alcoholic drink. If you are **on the booze** you are drinking heavily.

booze artist A heavy drinker.

booze bus A mobile police unit used for random breath testing.

booze cruise A water cruise during which many pubs are visited.

boozer 1. The pub or a club. 2. Someone who drinks booze.

booze up A prolonged drinking session.

bo-peep To take a sly look at something.

bored shitless To be very bored.

bore it up To give someone a lot of angst.

born loser Someone who is continually unsuccessful.

borrie Slang for excrement, mainly used in Victoria.

boss cocky The boss or the top bloke in an organisation.

bottle 1. To strike someone or knock them over. 2. If you **hit the bottle** you are about to start drinking and if you are **on the bottle** means you are drinking.

bottle blonde Someone with hair that has been dyed blonde.

bottle-oh or **bottlo** 1. The bottle shop or liquor store. 2. A person whose job was to collect used bottles for cleaning and re-sale. 3. A type of glass marble.

bottler A term used to express approval or admiration, e.g. 'You little bottler'.

bottoms up Emptying the beer glass.

botty A child's word, often used by adults, to describe the bottom.

bowlo Abbreviation of bowling club.

box 1. A television set. 2. If something is **out of the box** then it is remarkable but if it is **nothing out of the box** it is not particularly exciting. 3. Slang term for the vagina.

box bandit A male who sleeps around a lot.

boxhead One who has a large, squarish head.

box monster A cask of wine.

box seat The best position, e.g. 'Australia's in the box seat in this Test'.

boys in blue The police force.

boy wonder Any man or boy with marvellous attributes but generally used ironically.

bozo A fool or a buffoon.

Brahms and Liszt Rhyming slang for being pissed or very drunk.

brain To hit someone hard on the head.

brain dead 1. Stupid. 2. Mentally exhausted.

brain explosion A brief fit of madness or stupid behaviour.

brasco Slang term for toilet.

brass 1. Money. 2. High ranking military officers.

brass monkey weather Extremely cold weather that is also said to be **cold enough to freeze the balls off a brass monkey**.

brass razoo A coin of negligible value, e.g. 'I haven't got a brass razoo'.

bread Money or earnings.

breadbasket Slang term for the stomach.

brekkie Abbreviation of breakfast.

brewer's droop Alcohol-induced sexual impotence in men.

brick Term used to describe someone who is honest, reliable and trustworthy.

brickie A bricklayer.

brickie's cleavage Top of the buttocks exposed when the pants or trousers are not sufficiently pulled up.

bridge To accidentally display underwear while wearing a skirt.

as **bright as a box of budgies** or **birds** Used to describe someone who is intelligent or smart and comes from the fact that birds are supposedly smarter than humans because they can fly.

bright spark Describes someone who is intelligent or a self-starter. Also used as a sarcastic term for someone who is foolish, e.g. 'He's a real bright spark'.

Britney A glass of beer, from the rhyming slang Britney Spears for beers.

bronzed Sun-tanned.

brothel Any room or place that is a mess.

Brown bomber or **blue bomber** A parking inspector. Also known as **sticker licker**, **grey meanie** or **grey ghost** depending on the colour of the uniform.

browneye Gesture of contempt in which one bends over and bares the bottom.

brownie point Scoring an imaginary point to gain you credit.

brown nose A crawler or someone who servilely does what is asked in order to please the boss.

brown sandwich A Queensland slang term for a bottle of beer.

brush-off Rejection of romantic or sexual advances.

bub 1. A baby or infant. 2. Affectionate name for a girlfriend, wife or daughter.

bubbler A water spout attached to a basin to quench the thirst. Also a **bubble tap**.

buck 1. A dollar. Originally an American term but now widely used in Australia. 2. Any man. 3. The bridegroom-to-be.

bucket What you do when you soundly criticise someone or something. In other words they have just been **bucketed** or **had the bucket tipped on them**.

Buckley's chance or **Buckley's** Having no chance at all. Possibly referring to an escaped convict William Buckley. The most commonly used phrases are 'He's got Buckley's' and 'You've got two chances — Buckley's and none'.

bucko A term of address for a male used in a slightly confrontational manner.

buck's night A male get-together held before the wedding for the bridegroom by his mates.

so **bucktoothed he/she could eat a watermelon through a barbed wire fence** A description for someone with protruding front upper teeth.

buddy or **bud** Generally a male friend or mate.

budgie An abbreviation of budgerigar.

budgie smugglers A slang term for Speedos, a brief form of Australian male swimwear. It is also used to describe male underwear.

bugalugs or **buggerlugs** A mock abusive term commonly used as a term of endearment.

bugger 1. Originally a person taking part in anal sex. 2. A contemptible or despicable person but now more generally a merely annoying person, e.g. 'He's a silly bugger'. 3. A mischievous person, e.g. 'He's a real little bugger'. To **play silly buggers** is to muck around. 4. A nuisance, difficulty or something unpleasant, e.g. 'That's a real bugger'. 5. An exclamation of disgust or annoyance, e.g. 'Ahh, bugger it'. 6. **bugger up** To ruin or to wreck, e.g, 'That's buggered'.

bugger about, **bugger around** or **buggerise around** To mess around or to waste time.

bugger-all Not much or nothing, e.g. 'He's done bugger-all today'.

buggered Exhausted, worn out or very tired.

buggered if I know Means you don't have a clue.

bugger me I'll be damned or with more force **bugger me dead**.

bugger off What you say to someone when you want them to leave.

buggery Used to intensify a statement, e.g. 'It hurts like buggery'.

bugle A euphemism for the nose. If something is **a bit on the bugle** it is very smelly.

bug rake A slang term for a hair comb.

builder's crack Bottom cleavage appearing above the top of the pants or shorts.

built For a woman this means curvaceous while for a bloke it means solid and thick set. Also **built like a tank** or **built like a brick shithouse**.

bulk A great many.

bull Nonsense, raving. An abbreviation of **bullshit** or **bulldust**.

Bullamakanka An imaginary remote town that could be anywhere in Australia.

bull artist or **bullshit artist** A person who habitually speaks rubbish.

bulldust A euphemism for bullshit.

bullet To be given the bullet is to be fired from your job.

bullet-head A person with a large, squarish head.

bullshit Nonsense or rubbish.

bum 1. The bottom or backside. Once considered to be a taboo word but is now in common usage such as in **bums on seats** or **as smooth as a baby's bum**. 2. A homeless person living on the streets. 3. To cadge, e.g. 'I'll have to bum a ride'. 4. To move idly about, e.g. 'I'm just bumming around today'. 5. Of poor quality or bad, such as **a bum deal**. 6. Anything that fails completely such as it has **died in the bum**.

bum around To do nothing in particular.

bum chum A homophobic term for one of a gay male couple.

bum floss A G-string or other items of skinny underwear.

bum fluff Light hair growing on the face of an adolescent male.

bummer A bad outcome or a big disappointment.

bum nut A chicken's egg.

bump and grind Sexual intercourse.

bumper 1. Something large or successful. 2. A cigarette butt.

bump off To kill someone.

bum rap An unjust or false conviction or an unfair assessment.

bum sniffer A derogatory term used by Aussie Rules people for rugby league or union people in reference to the packing of scrums.

bum steer Incorrect advice or information given to someone.

bunch of fives If someone offers you a bunch of fives you'd better duck as it refers to a punch.

bundy 1. The Queensland town of Bundaberg and its famous product Bundaberg Rum. 2. A time clock used to record the arrival and departure of employees, thus to **bundy on** or to **punch the bundy** is to start work and to **bundy off** is to finish.

bung 1. Not in good working order, broken, not functioning, or injured. 2. To put or place quickly, e.g. 'Bung that pie in the oven'.

bunger 1. A large, exploding firecracker. 2. A cigarette.

bunghole 1. A slang word for cheese, as first used by Aussie soldiers in World War I. 2. Slang for the mouth.

bung it on To behave badly or temperamentally. Also to put on airs and graces.

bung on To hold a party or event, e.g. 'We'll bung on a barbie for her birthday'.

bung on an act To make a big fuss over nothing.

bun in the oven A baby in the womb.

bunk To run away or depart.

Bunker, the Another name for Parliament House in Canberra.

bunny 1. A fool or someone who is easily duped. 2. Someone who accepts responsibility for a situation. 3. A poor batsman in cricket.

bunny-hop or **kangaroo hop** To release the clutch of a manual car unevenly so that it moves forward in a series of jerky movements.

buns Slang term for the buttocks.

bunyip A mythical creature of an amphibious nature inhabiting rivers, pools and billabongs. From the Wembawemba Aboriginal language of Victoria and southern NSW.

bunyip aristocracy A derogatory term for what passes for peerage in Australia.

'burbs An abbreviated form of the suburbs.

burl 1. To attempt or have a go, e.g. 'I'll give it a burl'. 2. To move along quickly, e.g. 'That car is burling down the street'.

burn 1. To drive at high speed. 2. To outplay an opponent.

burn off To drive off at speed from traffic lights in order to beat someone else.

burnout To accelerate in a car so that the back wheels spin at high speed and cause as much smoke as possible.

burnt offering Overcooked or burnt food, especially that cooked at barbecues.

burr up To become angry after being stirred up.

burst a blood vessel To become agitated or overly excited.

bus Another name for a motor vehicle, especially when giving a lift to someone, e.g. 'The bus is leaving now'.

bush 1. The country as opposed to the city; anywhere that is largely uncultivated or unsettled. To **go bush** is to visit the country or unsettled areas. 2. Pubic hair.

bush banana Excrement.

bush bashing or **scrub bashing** To go off-road in a vehicle in the bush.

bush bellows A hat used to fan a camp fire.

bush blow The ejection of mucus from one nostril while closing the other with a finger. Also called a **bush hanky** or a **bushman's hanky**.

bush chook A slang term for an emu.

bushed 1. Exhausted or worn out. 2. Lost in the bush.

bushfire blonde A redhead.

bushie Anyone who lives in or comes from the country or a person wise to the ways of the bush.

bush lawyer Someone without legal qualifications but who has a general knowledge of the law and is crafty in applying it. Also known as a **Barcoo lawyer**.

bushman's breakfast To urinate and have a good look around.

bush mechanic Someone skilled at keeping old cars going in the outback without having all of the latest equipment.

bush oyster The product of a bush blow.

bush pig A term of contempt directed at a woman or girl, implying that they are ugly, unpleasant and rough.

bushranger 1. A highwayman. 2. Any unscrupulous person who rips you off.

bush telegraph The country gossip network or the outback rumour mill. Also called the **bush wireless**.

bush tele A camp fire or the stars. In other words, what you watch at night in the bush.

bush tucker 1. Simple country fare 2. Food gathered from nature in the bush.

Bush Week A fictitious week when country people come to town. It is used in the rhetorical phrase 'What do you think it is — Bush Week?' In other words, don't take me for a fool.

bushwhacker A person living in the bush, also a bushie.

business end The serious or dangerous part of something, such as 'The mouth's the business end of a snake' or 'We're at the business end of the conference'.

bust To catch someone doing something illegal or wrong.

bust a gut To work relentlessly.

buster 1. A heavy fall. 2. A strong wind.

busy as a one-armed paper-hanger in a gale A phrase used when you are really busy. Also **busy as a bee with a bum full of honey**, **busier than a one-armed bill-poster in a stiff breeze**, **busier than a one-armed bricklayer in Baghdad**, **busier than a one-armed taxi driver with crabs**, or **busier than a one-legged man in an arse-kicking contest**.

butch A masculine woman.

butcher 1. A small beer glass found in SA. 2. To spoil or wreck something is to **butcher it**.

butcher's canary A slang term for a blowfly, as flies are attracted to meat and could be considered to be pets of butchers.

butcher's 1. To take a look at something. An abbreviation of the rhyming slang of **butcher's hook** for look. 2. Feeling ill. Abbreviation of the rhyming slang butcher's hook for crook.

butt The buttocks or the backside.

butthole surfer A homosexual man.

buy A bargain, e.g. 'That was the buy of the year'.

buzz 1. A telephone call 2. An exhilarating feeling.

buzz box A derogatory term for a cheap, small car that has been hotted up.

buzz off To urge someone to leave or depart, e.g. 'Why don't you buzz off?'

by jingoes To be certain or sure, e.g. 'You can bet on that by jingoes'.

BYO Abbreviation of 'bring your own' which means to bring your own meat or alcohol or anything else that the host is not supplying.

by the living Harry By God!

C

Cabbage Garden An old derisive nickname for Victoria, making fun of the state's small land area. Also called the **Cabbage Patch** or **Cabbage State**. A Victorian was a **Cabbage Gardener, Patcher** or **Stater.**

cab sav An often used abbreviation of cabernet sauvignon wine.

cack 1. Another word for excrement as used in the insult 'Go dip your eye in hot cocky cack'. 2. The act of defecation, e.g. 'The baby cacked its nappy'. To **cack the corduroys** is to be scared enough to poo yourself. 3. Something that is extremely funny and that is said to make you **cack yourself laughing**, e.g. 'He was so funny I just cacked myself'.

cack-handed or **cacky-handed** Slang for left handed.

cackle berry Slang for a hen's egg.

cactus Someone or something that is not working, ruined or wrecked, e.g. 'That engine is cactus, mate'. Someone who is in trouble is said to be 'in the cactus', referring to the dreaded prickly pear which once covered much of Australia.

Cadbury A person who cannot handle their drink, referring to an old Cadbury advertising catch phrase of 'a glass and a half'.

cake-eater An effeminate male, or a sissy.

cakehole A slang expression for the mouth.

call 1. A decision to act in a certain way. Calls usually fall into three categories — the **bad call**, the **good call** or the **big call**. The bad call can also be called a dodgy call and is often used when someone does something particularly stupid or goes against the obvious choice. A good call is made when you do something that proves to be right and a big call is when you go out on a limb with a prediction. 2. A verb used to make a decision about something, e.g. 'It was hard to call'.

call a spade a shovel The Aussie way of calling a 'spade a spade' or calling it as it is.

call God on the big white telephone To vomit into the toilet bowl.

call it a day To finish up the job.

call of nature The natural urge to go to the toilet.

calorie-attack A session where too much is eaten.

camel bite A sharp and painful blow to the skin, usually to the top of someone's bare legs, and made by using a cupped hand. The term is most commonly used in WA with the most common term used in the rest of Australia being **horse bite**.

camel driver An unsuccessful jockey in horse racing.

camel jockey A racist term used to describe someone from the Middle East.

camel's piss Beer that doesn't taste too good.

came out like a shower of shit Very fast.

camo Abbreviation of camouflage.

camp 1. Describes an effeminate male or a homosexual, especially in an exaggerated way but has now been largely replaced by gay. **Camp as a row of tents** describes someone who is obviously gay. 2. To **camp somewhere** is to stay for a while.

camp oven A cast-iron pot for cooking on a camp fire.

can 1. Slang term for the toilet. 2. Another term for jail or prison. 3. To be dismissed from a job. 4. A measure of distance that refers to the distance travelled while consuming a can of beer, e.g. 'It was a three-can trip'.

canary Another term for a yellow defect notice stuck to a car window and used predominantly in Victoria.

cancer stick A derogatory term for a cigarette.

cane 1. To beat severely in a competition, e.g. 'He copped a real caning'. 2. To treat harshly or roughly.

caned Description of someone who is under the influence of alcohol or drugs.

cane it To drive fast or accelerate sharply.

cane toad A player for the Queensland team in State of Origin rugby league contests and often used to describe any Queenslander.

canned Drunk.

can you keep one down? Another way of asking someone if they want a beer.

can't get peacocks out of emu eggs This saying refers to breeding or imperfect source material.

can't make a silk purse out of a sow's ear The inability to make something inferior appear to be of good quality.

cap Abbreviation of cappuccino.

caper A word with many meanings. It can refer to an occupation or job, e.g. 'What caper are you in?', or it can refer to behaviour or to whatever is going on.

captain Someone buying the drinks.

Captain Cook Rhyming slang for look, also shortened to captains.

carbie Abbreviation of carburettor.

carcass Referring to the body, e.g. 'Move your carcass'.

card-carrying Certified. A way of describing someone who is totally dedicated to a cause.

cardi or **cardie** Abbreviation of cardigan.

cardies Poker machines that display playing cards.

cark it Slang term meaning to die and can be used for humans or machines.

carn An Aussie sporting fan's cry, e.g. 'Carn the reds'. It is a shortened form of 'come on'.

carpet grubs Slang term for children.

carrot top A red-headed person.

carry on like a pork chop To make a fuss about nothing.

carry the can To bear the responsibility for something that has gone wrong. Refers to carrying a sanitary can.

case Someone who is a little strange and eccentric, e.g. 'That bloke's a real case'.

cashed up Someone who has money at hand.

cash in your chips To die.

castle 1. The stumps in a game of cricket. 2. A home, as referred to in the expression 'Your home is your castle'.

cat 1. A gay man. 2. If you **look like something the cat dragged in**, you look untidy or unkempt.

cat burying shit, as busy as a, To be very busy.

catch and kiss 1. Derogatory name for soccer and generally used by fans of the other football codes. 2. A schoolyard game.

catch forty winks To have a short sleep.

cat fight A fight or dispute between two women.

cathedral underpants Very tight underpants that 'have no ball room'.

cat nap To take a short sleep.

cat's eye 1. A term for a three-corner jack. 2. A type of playing marble. 3. Small reflective light on the road.

cat's piss, as mean, or weak, as, A description of someone that is mean, stingy or uncharitable.

cat's pyjamas Something considered to be very good or 'the bee's knees'.

cattle dog Rhyming slang for a catalogue.

cattle tick Rhyming slang for a person of the Catholic faith.

caught short A desperate need to go to the toilet.

cellar dwellers Any team at the bottom of the competition ladder.

the **Centre** The inland part of Australia.

cert Something that is certain to happen, e.g. 'That horse is a dead cert'.

chaff Another term for money.

chainsaw head A derogatory term for someone with orthodontic braces on their teeth.

chalkie Commonly used description of a teacher.

champ 1. Shortened form of champion. 2. A form of address among men, e.g. 'How ya goin' champ?'

champers Champagne.

chances In your dreams or not likely.

chap A bloke or a fellow.

chardie Abbreviation of chardonnay.

charge 1. To get a thrill or a kick out of something. 2. An alcoholic drink. To **charge up** is to get drunk.

charlie 1. A girl or woman. Shortened from the rhyming slang Charlie Wheeler for sheila. 2. A Viet Cong soldier in the Vietnam war and derived from the military signals code Victor Charlie for VC.

charlies Slang term for breasts.

chase up a cow To find a dry spot outdoors usually with sexual activities in mind.

chasey A schoolyard game also known as **tag**, **chasings**, **tip** or **tips**, **tiggy** or **tig**.

chateau cardboard Another name for a wine cask.

chatterbox 1. A very talkative person. 2. A children's handmade fortune telling device manipulated by the thumb and index finger. Also called a chimper-chomper.

chat up Talking to someone with the aim of impressing them.

cheap as chips Something that is very inexpensive.

cheap at half the price Ironic expression for something that is not cheap at all.

cheapies A shortened form of cheap thrills, something that is pleasing or excites and which is inexpensive.

cheapo Derogatory expression for something that is inexpensive and of poor quality.

cheat stick A resting stick in a game of pool.

checkout chick A female working at a supermarket or discount department store cash register.

to **check the plumbing** To go to the toilet.

check you later A 'cool' way of saying goodbye or 'see you later'.

cheerio 1. A friendly form of saying goodbye. 2. A cocktail frankfurt in Queensland and northern NSW.

cheers, big ears A jocular toast made regardless of the size of the ears.

cheese and kisses Rhyming slang for 'the missus' or wife.

cheesed off To be very annoyed, e.g. 'I was really cheesed off with him'.

cheesy 1. Cool but only because it is uncool, e.g. 'She likes cheesy clothes'. 2. Smelly.

cheesy grin A fake smile.

chemo Shortened form of chemotherapy.

chequed up Having lots of cash after receiving a pay cheque.

cherry 1. A brand new red cricket ball. 2. The red mark made on a cricket bat after it hits a new ball or makes a strong stroke. 3. A woman's virginity.

chew and spew Description of takeaway food, e.g. 'Let's have chew and spew for dinner'.

chewie Shortened form for chewing gum.

chewie on your boot A cry made with the intention of putting off a footballer about to take a kick.

chew out To scold someone.

chew someone's ear To talk to someone at length in order to make a point.

chew the fat To have a discussion with someone.

chiack, **chiak** or **chiack** To taunt or tease.

chick A young woman.

chickenfeed An insignificant amount of money.

chicken out To opt out of doing something without real reason or in a cowardly way.

chickenshit Something that is worthless or pathetic.

chick flick A movie that appeals mainly to women.

chick magnet A male attractive to many females.

chick thing Something that only females are concerned with.

chicky babe A term of familiar address from a male to a young woman and usually in a joking manner. Also used by men to describe an attractive young woman.

chief cook and bottle washer Someone who is both in charge and doing everything.

Chinaman 1. A left-handed bowler's googly delivery in cricket. 2. A term used to describe any male from China. If you've had some bad luck it is common to say that you **must have killed a Chinaman** as it is traditionally considered to bring bad luck.

china plate Rhyming slang for mate and often shortened to **china**, e.g. 'How ya goin' my old china?'

Chinese burn A form of torture among schoolchildren whereby the victim's wrist is grabbed in both hands and the skin is twisted in opposite directions.

Chinese cut An inside edge in cricket that travels just wide of leg stump. Also called a French cut.

Chinese safety boots Thongs. Also called **Japanese safety boots** or **Japanese riding boots.** These are ironic terms as they are often made in Asia from cheap rubber and/or plastic and are unsuitable as footwear for safety or riding.

chinless wonder A feeble male.

chinwag To have a good chat with someone.

chip To reprimand someone, e.g. 'I was chipped for being late'. To **spit chips** is to vent anger.

chip on the shoulder To bear a grudge against someone.

chippie Slang term for a carpenter because they spend most of their time chipping away at bits of wood.

chisel 1. An old paper $5 note that bore an image of colonial welfare worker Caroline Chisholm, also called a **Chisholm**. 2. To cheat or swindle.

chock-a-block Very full, e.g. 'The garbage bin was chock-a-block'. Also **chockers** or **chock-full**.

chockie Abbreviation of chocolate. Also **chockie bikkies**, meaning chocolate biscuits.

chocoholic A person addicted to chocolate.

chocolate frog Rhyming slang for wog, a person of Mediterranean background.

choice Commonly used by young people to describe something that they really like, e.g. 'That's a choice dress'.

choke To fail due to lack of nerve.

choke a brown dog To be repulsive.

choke a darkie To defecate.

choko pie A derogatory term for a McDonald's apple pie based on the incorrect belief that they are made with apple-flavoured chokoes.

chompers The teeth.

choof off The act of leaving or asking someone to leave, e.g. 'It's getting late, I think I'll choof off'.

chook 1. An oft used, classic Australian term for a chicken, live or dead. **How's ya muvver's chooks** was a common greeting used years ago but now seldom heard. To **run around like a headless chook** is to behave erratically. If you wish ill luck on someone you may say **I hope your chooks turn into emus and kick your dunny down**. 2. A term for a woman but usually used to describe an older woman, e.g. 'She's a nice old chook'. 3. A silly person or a fool can be described as a **silly chook**. 4. Another description used of a cowardly person, similar to chicken.

chook chaser A derogatory term for a trail bike or small motorcycle or a person who rides one.

chook raffle A fund-raising raffle with chickens as the prizes.

chop 1. A share or a cut, e.g.'I'm in for a chop'. 2. To **get the chop** is to be fired from a job. 3. Something that is no good, as in **not much chop**. 4. A young person's code for asking whether a friend had sex. 5. A larrikin or dickhead.

chop and change To change repeatedly.

chop chop Hurry up.

chopper 1. Shortened form of helicopter. 2. A motorcycle with wide handlebars. 3. An old cow sold to be chopped up for pet food.

choppers Slang term for teeth.

chow 1. Slang term for food 2. A racist term for a Chinese person. Also ching.

chow down To eat with gusto.

chrissie Abbreviation of Christmas.

christen To use something for the first time.

Christmas Used in various slang expressions. **Regular as Christmas** Something that occurs regularly. **Done up like a Christmas tree** Overdressed. To **think you are Christmas** is to have a high opinion of yourself. If you have a lot of luck then **all your Christmases have come at once**.

Christmas hold or **grip** The grasping or grabbing of one's testicles, as in a handful of nuts.

chrome dome Derogatory term for a bald person.

chronic Someone or something that is really bad.

chuffed To be happy with something.

chuck 1. To vomit. This can be the act of vomiting or the vomit itself. 2. To throw. 3. To do or perform something. For instance to **chuck a U-ie** is to do a U-turn while to **chuck a left** or **right** is to turn in that direction. To **chuck a lap** is to drive around the block or along a street repeatedly as a form of entertainment. To **chuck a sickie** is to take the day off work while to **chuck a wobbly**, a **spaz**, **mental**, **willy**, **mickey or nana** is to lose your cool. 4. To stop doing something or to **chuck it in**.

chucker In cricket, someone who throws the ball instead of bowling it.

chuck in To give up or throw in the towel.

chuck off at To have a go at someone.

chug To have a drink. **Chug-a-lug** is a bout of drinking.

chum A friend or a mate. To **chum up with** someone is to befriend them.

chump 1. The head. 2. A blockhead.

chunder To vomit or the vomit itself. From rhyming slang 'Chunder Loo', or spew, and referring to a cartoon character drawn by Norman Lindsay. A **chunderer** is someone who is always spewing.

chunderdaks Someone with their pants pulled right up.

chunderous Revolting or unpleasant.

ciggie A cigarette.

cinch Something that is very easy or presents no problems, e.g. 'That exam was a cinch'.

circle work Doing burnouts in a vehicle or motorcycle in a circle.

City of Churches Adelaide.

city slicker A person living in a large city.

clacker The backside, or the female genitals.

clackers False teeth.

clancy An overflow or spillage of petrol. From the Banjo Paterson poem *Clancy of the Overflow*.

clanger A faux pas, a lie or a big blunder.

clap Any form of venereal disease.

clapped out Old, worn out or exhausted, e.g. 'The car was clapped out'.

clappers Something that goes really fast, e.g. 'That car goes like the clappers'.

clap trap Nonsense, e.g. 'What a load of clap trap'.

claret A metaphor for blood and commonly used in sport.

classic Something that is excellent.

Clayton's Fake or false. This word came into common usage in the 1980s in conjunction with an advertising campaign for Clayton's, a non-alcoholic drink, which was advertised as 'the drink you have when you're not having a drink'. It is now used to describe anything that exists in name only.

clean Free from addiction or disease.

cleaner-upper Someone responsible for cleaning up.

cleanskin 1. An unbranded or unlabelled wine. 2. An unbranded animal. 3. A novice at something. 4. Someone without a police record.

clear as mud Used to describe something that is confusing, e.g. 'That's as clear as mud'.

clear the cobwebs 1. To have sex. 2. To use something that hasn't been used for a while.

clever dick A show-off.

click Slang term for a kilometre, also spelt **klick**.

clink Slang term for prison.

clip A mild form of punishment dealt with the open hand.

clobber 1. Clothes or gear, as in 'to put on your best clobber'. 2. To bash or hit somebody.

clock 1. A speedometer or odometer. To **clock it** is to drive a car until its odometer has returned to the initial position of all zeros. 2. To hit someone.

clock-watcher An employee who spends most of their time keeping an eye on the clock for the end of the day.

clodhoppers Large feet or large boots.

close, but no cigar An indication that someone has made a good guess or a good answer but it is still not correct. If the guess is correct the phrase is **give the man/woman a cigar**.

clout To hit someone or something hard.

clubber A person who frequents nightclubs.

clubbie A member of a surf-lifesaving club. **Clubbies** is a nickname for the Speedos, or swimwear briefs, usually worn by lifesavers.

clucky Feeling maternal or broody and often used to describe people who may be longing for children of their own.

clued up Someone who is well informed.

cluey Smart or well informed.

clumsy as a duck in a ploughed paddock Used to describe someone who is extremely clumsy.

clunky 1. Unsophisticated. 2. Not running smoothly.

coalie A dock worker, or wharfie, employed to load or unload coal.

coals to Newcastle Used to describe something that it pointless or useless because coal is mined in the Newcastle region.

coathanger 1. Term of endearment for the Sydney Harbour Bridge. 2. A head-high tackle in rugby league or rugby union.

cobber 1. A mate, friend, pal or buddy. 2. A popular, hard lolly or sweet with a centre of thick caramel coated in milk chocolate.

cobblers 1. Nonsense, e.g. 'That's a load of old cobblers'. 2. The testicles.

cock 1. The penis. An age-old reference to a rooster being called a cockerel. 2. A disliked or despised male. 3. A term of friendly address in Tasmania. A complete stranger may say to you in Tasmania 'G'day cock'.

cockatoo Someone who keeps watch for the law during an illegal activity, or a lookout.

cockeyed bob A particularly violent, sudden and short-lived storm or squall. The term is used mainly in WA and the Northern Territory. First recorded in 1894 and may be a mispronunciation of the Aboriginal word *kikobor.*

cock head A ratbag or a disliked person.

cockie Abbreviation of cockroach.

cockroach 1. A player for the NSW State of Origin rugby league team and, therefore, anyone from NSW. 2. A hard lump of brown sugar.

cocksucking Dreadful or awful and usually used as an intensifier.

cockteaser A woman who leads a man on and then leaves him in the lurch. Also known as a pricktease.

cock up To make a mistake or something that has gone wrong.

cocky 1. Abbreviation of cockatoo or other parrot. After a big night out you will often wake up with a **mouth like the bottom of a cocky's cage**, or full of grit. 2. A farmer. The farmer's individual specialty is often put in front of this term, e.g. a cow cocky, a cane cocky, a sheep cocky, etc. 3. A lock of hair sticking out, like a cockatoo's crest.

cockylora A schoolyard chasings game, also called **British bulldog**.

cocky on the biscuit tin A description of the Arnott's Biscuits logo and used as a metaphor to denote being left out, or being on the outside looking in.

cocky's delight Treacle or golden syrup. Also **cocky's joy**. These were generally not as expensive as jam and were, therefore, more affordable for hard-working farmers, or cockies, who considered them to be a real treat.

coconut A derisive term for any native of the Pacific Islands or person with dark skin.

code monkey A computer programmer.

cods Euphemism for the testicles.

codswallop Absolute nonsense.

coffin nail 1. Cigarette. 2. To **put another nail in the coffin** is to make another notch against someone after they have done something wrong or disagreeable.

Coffs Shortened name for the NSW coastal town of Coffs Harbour.

coin slot Bottom cleavage appearing above the top of pants or shorts.

coit 1. The anus. 2. An annoying person.

Coke bottle glasses Spectacles with thick lenses.

cold as a witch's tit Something or someone that is very cold. Also **colder than a mother-in-law's kiss**.

coldie A cold can, bottle or glass of beer and now just used as an alternative to the word beer, e.g. 'I think I'll crack open a coldie'. Also **cold one**.

collect A winning bet, as in to collect.

Collins Street cocky In Victoria, a person who lives in Melbourne but owns a country property, often as a way of avoiding tax. In NSW they are **Pitt Street farmers** and in Queensland **Queen Street bushies**.

collywobbles 1. An upset or queasy stomach. 2. A feeling of uneasiness or nervousness about something. 3. In reference to nervousness it refers to the poor record of the Collingwood AFL team which has only won three premierships since World War II but has been runner-up 11 times.

combo Any combination of things.

combs and cutters Knives and forks.

come a cropper 1. To fall heavily. 2. To fail or have misfortune. Also to **come a gutser**.

come in on the grouter To arrive after the work has been finished either through luck or contrivance. Laying the grout is the last job done when tiling and the grouter is the last person to work on the job.

come in, spinner! 1. A call made in the gambling game of two-up to indicate that all bets have been laid and it is time to spin the coins. 2. Used to inform someone they have been duped or had.

come off it Be reasonable.

come on to To seduce someone.

come out To publicly admit homosexuality.

come to blows To start fighting.

come up and see my etchings An excuse to invite a person home in order to seduce them.

comic cuts Rhyming slang for the guts or stomach.

commie Slang term for a communist or leftist supporter. Also **commo**.

common as dog shit Something that is very common.

compassionate as a starving shark To have no sympathy at all.

compo Abbreviation of worker's compensation, e.g. 'He was off work on compo'.

con 1. Shortened form of confidence trick. To swindle someone. Also **con job**. 2. A prisoner or ex-prisoner.

con artist A swindler. Also **con man**.

conchie Anyone who is conscientious.

conehead A dope addict.

conk Another term for the nose.

conk out To break down. Most commonly used in reference to mechanical items but also if someone collapses from exhaustion.

connie 1. A tram conductor. 2. A small stone for throwing. 3. A playing marble.

continental A fete or similar function held as a fundraiser. To **not give a continental** is not to care at all.

control freak A person who likes to keep in control of every situation and detail.

coodies Head lice. Also **cooties**.

coods The testicles.

cooee The great Australian bush cry. To not answer the cry of cooee is un-Australian, that is if you are **within cooee** of someone. If you are close to achieving a goal you are also **within cooee** of that goal but if you are far from an achievement you are **not within cooee**.

cook To go along well, e.g. 'She is really cooking in her new job'.

cooking with gas To be doing very well at something.

cook up To concoct something.

cool 1. Suave, up to date, stylish. 2. Excellent. 3. All right or okay. 4. Composed. To **lose your cool** is to become uncomposed.

cool as a cucumber To be very calm or unruffled.

cool bananas All right or groovy.

cooler Prison.

coon and goon night A wine and cheese night with Coon being a brand of cheese.

coot 1. A silly person. 2. A man and generally an old man, e.g. 'He's a real old coot'.

cop 1. Shortening of **copper**, or police officer. 2. To catch someone out while they are doing something illegal, e.g. 'Johnny was copped wagging school'. 3. To get or receive, e.g. 'She copped a hefty fine'. 4. To look at, e.g. 'Take a cop at that'. 5. To make a profit, e.g. 'He could sell it and make a cop out of it'.

cop it To be punished.

cop it sweet To accept or to put up with something or someone, albeit grudgingly, e.g. 'I copped it sweet'.

cop out To opt out of something in a cowardly manner.

copper's nark A police informant.

cop shop A police station.

copspeak Police jargon.

cop the lot To suffer multiple misfortune at the one time.

cop you later Another way of saying 'See you later'.

cords Shortened form for corduroy trousers.

corker Something really good, e.g. 'That meal was a real corker'.

cornstalk A derisive nickname for a person from NSW.

cossie or **cozzie** Slang for a swimming costume or bathers.

cot Bed, e.g. 'It's time to hit the cot'.

cot case Someone who drinks to the point where all they can do is crash into bed. Also can be used for someone who is exhausted or incapacitated.

couch potato An inactive person who is generally found in front of the television.

cough up a lung A severe coughing fit.

could crack a flea on it Of your stomach after having eaten well.

could eat the crotch out of a low-flying duck To be extremely hungry. Other sayings are **could eat a horse and chase the rider** and **could eat a horse if you took its shoes off**.

couldn't fight your way out of a wet paper bag Someone who is weak or puny. Also **couldn't spread marge on a Sao**, in reference to the popular Australian biscuit.

couldn't pull a greasy stick out of a dead dog's arse Description of someone who is incompetent. Other examples are **couldn't organise sex in a brothel**, **couldn't organise a root in a brothel**, **couldn't organise a piss-up in a brewery**, **couldn't get a kick in a stable**, **couldn't pick a winner in a two-horse race**, **couldn't organise a fart in a curry house**, **couldn't sell beer to a drover**, **couldn't catch a fly in a country dunny**, **couldn't pour water from a boot with instructions on the heel**, **couldn't sell ice-cream in hell**, **couldn't train a choko vine to grow up a dunny wall**, and **couldn't find his dick with both hands**.

counterjumper A salesperson at a counter.

counter lunch A meal served at lunch time in a pub.

the **country** The parts of a sportsground that are far away from the action.

country cousin 1. A term used by people living on the coast to describe anyone from the country. Also **country bumpkin**. 2. Rhyming slang for a dozen.

country dunny A traditional country toilet that stands by itself in a small shed away from the home. To be **all alone like a country dunny** is to be alone.

country mile To win by a great distance.

a couple of lamingtons short of a CWA meeting Lacking a full quota of intelligence. Also **a couple of sandwiches short of a picnic** or **a couple of alps short of a range**.

cove An old fashioned term for a man, e.g. 'He was a real flash cove'.

cover your arse To protect yourself.

cow 1. A contemptible person. 2. A bad-tempered woman, e.g. 'She was a cranky old cow'. 3. Something unpleasant. 4. An unpleasant woman or a bitch.

coward's castle Parliament. Particularly used when politicians use parliamentary privilege to vilify others.

cowboy 1. An unreliable and poor worker who tends to cut corners, therefore not completing the job properly. 2. A business person who cuts corners. 3. In rural areas, a man employed to milk cows.

cow cocky A small-scale cattle farmer or a dairy farmer.

cow corner That part of a cricket field over mid wicket and so called because it was such a remote fielding location that cows could graze there.

cow juice Milk.

cow-pat lotto or **lottery** A fundraising competition in which a cow is placed in a cleared paddock divided into numbered squares and raffled off with the winner decided by the fall of the first cow-pat.

crack 1. To attempt something. 2. To open something. Most commonly used in reference to opening a beer. 3. To obtain. 4. The anal cleft. 5. To gain unauthorised access to a computer or its software.

crack a fat To get an erection.

cracker 1. A firework. 2. Excellent, e.g. 'That goal was a real cracker'. 3. Money, e.g. to **not have a cracker** is to be broke and **not worth a cracker** is worthless.

crackers Someone who has gone insane or who does something particularly stupid.

crack it To be successful.

crack on to To make a pass at someone or to woo them into bed.

cradle snatcher Someone going out with a much younger person.

cranking Excellent, hot or firing.

crank out To perform forcefully or to play music loudly.

crank up To stir into action.

crap 1. Excrement or the act of defecation. 2. Junk, rubbish or worthless. Also **crappy**. 3. Nonsense. 4. To be scared, as in 'I was crapping myself'. 5. An intensifier, e.g. 'He beat the crap out of me'.

crap on To talk nonsense at length.

crapper A toilet.

craptastic Hopeless or crap.

crap wrap Toilet paper.

crash 1. To get into a party uninvited. 2. To sleep over. 3. To collapse from exhaustion.

crash and burn To collapse from exhaustion or to fail miserably.

crash-hot Something that is really good or someone who is good looking. If you are **not feeling crash-hot**, you don't feel well.

crash out 1. To suddenly fall asleep. 2. To be beaten in a contest.

crate A dilapidated vehicle, e.g. 'Haven't you got rid of that old crate yet?'

crater face Someone with an acne-scarred face.

crawl To pander to someone and do whatever it takes to please them.

crawler Someone who will do whatever it takes to please the boss or someone in authority.

cray Shortened form of crayfish.

crayfish 1. A $20 note, taken from the note's colour. 2. A marine rock lobster in Tasmania, SA and NSW. 3. A colloquial name for the freshwater yabby. 4. An old slang term meaning to back down like a coward.

cream To beat up in a fight. Also **creamed** A team or an individual who is well beaten.

cred To have credibility.

crikey A great Australian expression of astonishment. It was originally a euphemism for exclaiming 'Christ!' and was brought to the attention of the world by the 'Crocodile Hunter' Steve Irwin.

crim Abbreviation of criminal.

cripes An expression of surprise. It was originally a euphemism for the blasphemous exclamation 'Christ'.

croak To die. Originated in Britain but has been used in Australia since 1812.

crock 1. A load of nonsense, e.g. 'He talks a load of old crock'. 2. A worn-out person or someone who is ill.

crock of shit Nonsense or lies.

cronk Dishonest or crooked.

crook 1. Something that is not good or inferior. 2. Not feeling well. 3. A criminal. 4. Angry or annoyed. To **go crook on** someone is to chastise them.

crook as Rookwood Someone who is extremely ill. Rookwood is a large cemetery in Sydney.

crooked Dishonest or illegal. Used in phrases like **as crooked as a dog's hind leg** and **so crooked he could hide behind a corkscrew**.

crooked on Angry with someone or something.

crool To ruin or spoil something.

the **Cross** Shortened name for the seedy Sydney suburb of Kings Cross.

cross-country ballet A derisive name for the game of Aussie Rules. **Cross-country wrestling** is also used derisively for rugby league or union.

crow The all-black birds of the Corvidae family. Used in slang phrases such as **the land where the crow flies backwards** or **where the crows fly backwards to keep the dust out of their eyes** meaning any remote place. **As the crow flies** refers to a straight line distance between two places. To **draw the crow** is to get the worst job. Then there's the great exclamation of surprise **stone the crows**.

crowd surf To be carried across the top of a packed crowd, particularly at rock concerts.

crow-eater A person from SA.

crown jewels The testicles. Also the **family jewels**.

crow peck A blow to the head with the knuckle of a bent middle or index finger.

crud Accumulated dirt, junk, nonsense or crap.

cruddy Inferior or unworthy.

crudville A bad place.

cruel To ruin or spoil something. To **cruel someone** is to ruin their chances.

cruet The head.

cruets The testicles.

cruise 1. To wander in a relaxed and cool manner. 2. To take it easy while doing something or to do it easy. 3. To go about with a view to finding a sexual partner.

cruising for a bruising Someone who is in imminent danger of being bashed.

crumb Used primarily in Aussie Rules to describe a loose ball on the fringe of a pack but now used in other ball sports to describe a loose ball on the ground. A player skilled at cleaning up the crumbs is a **crumber** or a **crumb gatherer**.

crumpet 1. A woman or man considered as a sexual object. 2. Sexual intercourse, as in 'I got a bit of crumpet last night'. 3. The head. 4. If something is **not worth a crumpet** it is worthless.

crunch time Time to make a critical decision.

crust A living or livelihood and commonly used in the expression 'What do you do for a crust?'

crusty 1. Dressed shabbily and unwashed. 2. Hung over.

cry Ruth or **call for Ruth** To vomit.

cuddy A horse.

Cunnamulla portmanteau Slang for a sugar bag used to hold your belongings. From the Queensland outback town of Cunnamulla, a regular stop for swagmen.

Cunnamulla tune-up A tune-up prank in which spark-plug leads are randomly swapped around.

cunning as a shithouse rat Someone who is sly or cunning.

cunning kick A secret pocket for concealing cash.

the **Cup** The Melbourne Cup horse race. **Cup day**, when the race is run, is the first Tuesday in November, **Cup eve** is the Monday night before it, **Cup week** is the week in which it falls and **Cup fever** strikes most Australians before the race. **Since Archer won the Cup** refers to any great length of time, the racehorse Archer being the first horse to win the cup, in 1861.

a cup of tea, a Bex and a good lie down is used to describe a method of relaxation. It was once popular among Australian housewives but is now used widely for anyone who needs to relax. It was originally an advertising line for the pain-killer Bex, which has since been banned owing to its addictive effect and its side effects, including renal disease.

cuppa A cup of tea or coffee.

curl the mo An old exclamation of surprise.

curly Nickname for a bald person.

curry To give someone a hard time, e.g. 'I really gave him a bit of curry'.

curry muncher A racist term for an Indian, Pakistani, Bangladeshi or Sri Lankan.

the **curse** Menstruation.

custard arm A player in cricket who cannot throw the ball very far.

custard brains A silly or stupid person.

cut 1. Under the influence of alcohol. 2. To dilute a drug with another substance. 3. Circumcised.

cutie 1. A sexy young woman and now also used in reference to men. 2. An attractive young child.

cutie-pie A woman or girl who is cute.

cut laps To drive repeatedly around the block or along a street, commonly done by bored youth.

cut lunch A light midday meal provided from home and often referring to sandwiches.

a cut lunch and a water bag How long something will take, particularly a journey.

cut out To pay a debt with work rather than money.

cuts A form of corporal punishment at school using a cane, which is now banned.

cut someone's lunch To make a move on or steal someone's else's girlfriend or partner. Also **to cut someone's else's grass**.

cut the mustard To be up to the task.

cut your lunch To fart, as in 'someone's cut their lunch'. Also 'open your lunch'.

C-word The dreaded C-word, the crudest word in the language. 1. Female external genitalia. 2. Crudely used to refer to women considered as sexual objects. 3. A contemptible man. 4. In a weak sense, used to describe any person and usually in a derogatory manner. 5. Sexual intercourse. 6. Something annoying or frustrating.

cyberbabe A cool female Internet user. Also called a **cyberchick**.

cyberdude A cool male Internet user. Also called a **cyberboy**.

cybersex Sexual interaction via the Internet.

D

d 1. A dozen longneck bottles of beer. 2. Abbreviation of detective, also **dee**.

dack To pull someone's pants down.

dacks or **daks** Slang term for trousers or pants. **Underdacks** is used to describe underwear while **trackie dacks** is used for tracksuit pants.

Dad 'n' Dave Rhyming slang for a shave. Taken from the quintessential Australian bush characters created by Steele Rudd in his book, *On Our Selection*.

dag 1. A lump of matted wool on a sheep's rear. 2. Anyone who is a little eccentric, stupid, uncool or lacks style is said to be a dag, or a **bit of a dag**.

dag bag A type of cotton bag usually slung over the shoulder.

dagdom The state of being a dag.

daggy Something that looks unkempt, is uncool or lacks style. Also **daggily** or **dagginess**.

dago An old racist term for anyone of Latin ethnic origin.

dags Comfortable old clothes usually worn around the house.

dagwood dog A battered sausage or frankfurt on a stick that is common at agricultural shows around Australia. Also called a **pluto pup** or in SA a **dippy dog**.

daisy chain Any group of people engaged in making love and forming some chain-like formation.

daisy-cutter A sporting term for any ball that skims just above the grass after being thrown, hit or kicked.

dak-dak A Volkswagen beetle. This comes from the noise the engine makes.

damage The cost or expense of something, e.g. 'What's the damage, mate?'

damper Unleavened bread traditionally made in the bush from flour and water and cooked in a camp oven on the coals of a campfire.

damp squib 1. A person who is a failure or a dud. 2. A racehorse or greyhound that starts well but finishes badly. A squib is a small firecracker.

D&M Abbreviation for a deep and meaningful conversation.

dancer Rhyming slang for cancer. Also **disco dancer**.

dangle the Dunlops To lower the landing gear of a plane.

dangly bits Male genitalia.

Dapto briefcase A localised name for a cask of wine. This expression is mainly used on the South Coast of NSW, where the town of Dapto is located, but has spread to other parts of the state. Also called a **Bellambi handbag** or **goon box**.

Dapto dog Rhyming slang for 'wog' or a person of Mediterranean background.

dark as three feet up a cow's arse Extremely dark.

darl A shortening of darling. Also **darls**.

Darlo The Sydney suburb of Darlinghurst.

dart A cigarette.

Darwin stubbie A very large beer bottle.

date The anus, or arse.

date packer A homophobic term for a homosexual man. Also **dung puncher**.

date roll Toilet paper.

dead A common slang word that means totally or completely, e.g. 'He was dead right'.

deadbeat 1. Someone who is down on their luck, such as a homeless person or a derelict. 2. Also a derogatory term used to describe anyone considered lazy, unmotivated and not contributing to society.

dead bird A certainty in horseracing as in a bird that has been shot and is in the bag.

dead centre or **dead heart** The region of Australia in the middle of the arid Northern Territory and so called because nothing much grows there.

dead cert Something that is an absolute certainty.

dead duck A flop or a failure. If you **look like a dead duck in a thunderstorm** then you look terrible.

dead fly biscuit A biscuit with a layer of dried fruit between two thin layers of sweet pastry. Also called a **squashed fly biscuit** or a **fly cemetery**.

dead from the neck up Describes someone who is lacking in intelligence or is considered to have no brains.

dead horse Rhyming slang for tomato sauce and great with a dog's eye (meat pie).

dead-leg 1. A cork of the thigh muscle. 2. Striking someone hard on the back of the upper leg is called a dead-leg.

deadly Fantastic, great or cool, e.g. 'She looked deadly in that skirt'. A word commonly used by Aboriginals in the 1980s but now also used by many non-Aboriginals, particularly in the Northern Territory.

deadly treadly Aussie slang for a bicycle.

dead marine A forlorn sight for a typical Aussie drinker — an empty beer stubby or long neck.

dead ringer An exact likeness of someone.

dead set For certain, without a doubt, no joke, honestly.

deadshit A contemptible person.

dead'un A dead person or a dead animal.

death adders in your pocket Used to describe someone who is miserly or stingy.

death bag The bladder from inside a wine cask.

death seat 1. The front passenger seat in a vehicle. 2. In a harness or trotting race the position taken up outside the leader during the race.

debag To remove someone's trousers as a joke.

deck 1. To deck someone is to knock them to the ground. 2. The pitch in a cricket game. 3. The top surface of a skateboard.

deener or **deaner** Another name for a shilling and used occasionally for 10 cents.

the **Deep North** Queensland or Far North Queensland. An analogy with America's Deep South.

deep throat 1. Fellatio. 2. An informer.

dekko or **decko** To have a look at something.

Delhi belly A case of severe diarrhoea suffering by people who travel to India.

deli Shortened form of delicatessen.

delish Another way of saying delicious.

delo Shortened form of delegate.

demo Abbreviation of demonstration. If you want to demonstrate against something you stage a demo.

demolish To eat greedily or to drink a lot, e.g. 'I could demolish a hamburger'.

dent knocker Slang term for a panel beater.

depot duck Slang for a crow at a rubbish tip. This term arose in the outback city of Broken Hill where it has been shortened to **depots**.

der A mock expression of fake stupidity, bewilderment or of the blatantly obvious.

der brain Fool or idiot.

derps Short for underpants.

derro or **dero** Short for derelict. The Aussie equivalent of wino. Also a **dope**.

desk wallah or **desk jockey** Derogatory name for an office worker.

desperado A person who is desperate for sex.

despo A desperate person.

devo Abbreviation of deviant.

DFE Dead fucking easy. Used to describe something that is absolutely easy.

DGs Dark glasses or sunglasses.

dial The face.

dice To throw away.

dick 1. The penis. 2. An annoying or disagreeable person. 3. Ruined or wrecked, e.g. 'The car has **had the dick'**. 4. Abbreviation for dictionary, e.g. 'Pass the dick'.

dick around To fool around.

dick bathers or **dick stickers** Men's Speedos, or swimming briefs. Also **dick-daks**, **dick pointers**, **dick togs** or **dick pokers**.

dick brain A fool.

dick eye An annoying person or a jerk. Also **dick flop** or **dickwit**.

dickhead A popular Australian expression of scorn for anyone who behaves in an idiotic, foolish or even disagreeable manner and particularly directed towards males. Also **dick face**, **dick nose** and **dick wad**.

Dickless Tracy A female police officer. Based on the cartoon crime-fighting character Dick Tracy.

dick rash An annoying person.

dick shit Someone a little more contemptible than a dickhead.

dicky 1. Something that is not functioning properly, which usually refers to body parts but can also mean mechanical items, e.g. 'He's got a dicky ankle'. 2. Stupid and annoying, e.g. 'Jumping down the stairs was a dicky thing to do'.

diddle To swindle or rip off someone.

diddly-squat Nothing or none.

diddums Used to indicate someone is being childish.

diddy The toilet.

didj or **didge** Abbreviation of didgeridoo.

died in the bum Something that has stopped working.

diesel dyke A butch lesbian.

diff 1. Abbreviation for difference and often used as 'What's the diff?' 2. The differential from a vehicle engine.

dig 1. To have a dig at someone is to be sarcastic towards them or to have a go at them. 2. To comprehend something or to 'get it'. 3. An innings in cricket.

digger A term originally used to describe a nineteenth-century gold miner and later affectionately used to typify the Australian soldier, a use that came about during World War I. Today it is also used to address someone in a friendly manner, particularly if you can't remember their name, similar to mate, e.g. 'G'day digger'.

dill A fool or someone who is not very bright. Also **dill-brain**.

dilly bag A small hand-woven bag used by Aboriginals. It has since been used to describe a toiletry bag and is now commonly used to describe any small bag.

dimmie A Victorian colloquialism for dim sim. These Australian–Chinese deep-fried treats once contained meat in Victoria and vegetables in NSW but now both kinds are generally available, although you usually have to specify which one you want.

dim sims The testicles.

din-dins A childish expression for dinner.

ding 1. A scratch or a small dent, e.g. 'The boot has a bit of a ding but apart from that the car's unmarked'. 2. A party and perhaps short for a wing ding. 3. The penis.

ding-a-ling A foolish or silly person.

dingbat A peculiar person or someone who is considered stupid.

dingbats Crazy or mad, e.g. 'She went dingbats'.

ding-dong 1. A strenuously contested fight or a 'barney'. 2. Powerful or extra strong, e.g. 'My missus has got a ding-dong headache'. 3. Complete or absolute, e.g. 'That bloke's a ding-dong lunatic'. 4. A simple or silly person, e.g. 'He's a bit of a ding-dong'.

dinger 1. A condom. 2. The anus.

dingle A small accident in which the vehicle suffers little damage. Also a **bingle**.

dingleberry A piece of excrement clinging to the hairs of the anus.

dingo A coward. To **turn dingo** on someone is to betray them.

dingo's breakfast To urinate and take a good look round, also a **bushman's breakfast**.

dink 1. To carry someone else on your bicycle, motorcycle or horse is to give them a dink. Also called **bar** or **barie** and **double** with state variations including **dinky** (WA and SA), **double-dink** (WA, Victoria and Tasmania), **dinky-double** (NSW and ACT) and **donkey** (SA). 2. An acronym for 'double income no kids', which describes couples who have two incomes but no children. 3. Abbreviation of dinkum.

dinkum Fair or genuine. Also **dinks**.

dinkum Aussie A genuine Australian who exhibits many of the traits of the Australian character.

dinky 1. Of small size. 2. A small tricycle.

dinky-di Very Australian. A common expression for something that is 'the genuine article' or fair dinkum.

dip out To opt out of doing something.

dippy dog The South Australian term for a battered sausage on a stick. Also **dagwood dog** or **pluto pup**.

dipshit A contemptible person.

dipstick A loser or an idiot.

dip your lid To raise your hat as a mark of respect. Often used in the phrase 'I dips me lid'.

dip your wick To have sex. A phrase usually used by men.

dirty 1. Angry or annoyed. 2. To **do the dirty** on someone is to cheat them. 3. An exaggeration, e.g. 'I saw a dirty big brown snake'.

Dirty Annie Slang term for Reschs Dinner Ale beer.

dirty deed 1. To do something underhanded. 2. Sexual intercourse.

To get the **dirty water off your chest** refers to having sexual intercourse after a long period without.

dish An attractive woman. It is also now used by women to describe attractive men.

dish licker Slang term for a racing greyhound. It can also be used to refer to any dog. To go to the dish lickers is to attend the dog races.

dishy Physically attractive.

dit A yarn or story as used in the phrase **spin a dit**. A teller of such stories is a **dit spinner**.

the **Ditch** 1. Used to describe the Tasman Sea between Australia and New Zealand. 2. Also used for Bass Strait between the mainland and Tasmania.

ditsy or **ditzy** An empty-headed woman.

ditty An amusing short yarn or poem.

dive A rundown place that is in good need of a spruce up.

divvy 1. A dividend. 2. To divide up money or payment is to **divvy it up**.

divvy van A police van for the transport of criminals.

dixie 1. A small container of ice-cream. Commonly used in Victoria and Tasmania. In SA it's called a **dandy**. 2. A small tin from which you eat, as used in the army.

do 1. A party or a function. 2. A hairdo. 3. To injure, e.g. 'She did her ankle while skipping'. 4. To spend all your money, e.g. 'I did my dough at the races'. 5. To have sex with. 6. To arrest someone or to book them for an offence, e.g. 'He got done for speeding'. 7. To drink or to have a meal with someone, e.g. 'I could do a beer'. 8. A compliment or praise, e.g. 'That new player, he'll do me'.

do a Bradbury To win unexpectedly as Aussie speed skater Steve Bradbury did at the 2002 Winter Olympics when all the other finalists fell, leaving Bradbury to come from behind and surprisingly win the race.

do a bunk To run away or flee the scene.

do a Melba To make a habit of returning from retirement and alluding to the opera singer Dame Nellie Melba.

do a runner To escape from something by running away.

dob 1. To inform or tattle-tale on someone is to **dob them in**. A common saying in Australia is 'I'll tell you if you promise not to dob'. 2. To kick a goal in Aussie Rules.

dobber Someone who informs or who tells tales about someone else to get them into trouble.

docile Describes someone who is not bright.

doco Abbreviation of documentary.

doctor A fresh sea breeze in WA that comes about in the afternoon during summer. Regional variations include **Fremantle doctor**, **Albany doctor** and **Esperance doctor**.

dodger A flyer or advertising leaflet.

dodgy Something or someone that is suspicious, underhanded or not to be trusted. Also something that is not reliable.

doer A hard and keen worker. It is usually a term of respect.

dog 1. A woman who is considered ugly or questionable. 2. A contemptible person. 3. An informer. To **turn dog** is to betray someone to the police or other authorities. 4. A prison warder. 5. A useless racehorse. 6. Something that is useless. 7. A dog used as a measurement of the cold, e.g. 'It was a three-dog night'. This refers to how many dogs you need to snuggle up to in order to keep warm.

dog and bone Rhyming slang for the telephone.

dog box Small, cramped quarters.

doggie A night shift, otherwise known as **dog watch**.

doggy do Dog excrement.

dog's balls Something that is very obvious, e.g. 'It stands out like dog's balls'.

dog's breakfast Describes a mess or something messy. Also called a **dog's dinner**.

dog's eye Rhyming slang for that great Aussie icon, the meat pie, and usually consumed with dead horse (tomato sauce).

dog squad Undercover police.

dog's vomit Food that doesn't taste too good.

do it on your ear To do something with ease. Another phrase that means the same is **I can do it on my shit-tub without getting a ring around my arse**.

do it tough To do something with a great deal of effort. Also describes difficult circumstances, as in 'Her husband died and she's doing it tough right now'.

dole Social security benefits.

dole bludger Someone who is content to live off social security payments without making any effort to get a job.

dolled up or to **doll up** Dressed smartly.

dolly catch An easy catch in cricket.

the **Don** A shortened name for Donald Bradman, Australia's greatest cricket batsman.

done like a dinner Describes a task when it is finished.

done up like a Christmas tree Overdressed or over-adorned.

dong To hit or strike something, e.g. 'He was donged on the head by the football'.

donga The bush or the outback, e.g. 'He's been out in the donga far too long.

donger 1. Euphemism for the penis. 2. A big stick used as a weapon.

donk 1. An engine. 2. Euphemism for the penis.

donkey To carry as a second passenger on a bicycle, motorcycle or horse. Used chiefly in SA.

donkey dick Describes the genitals of a well-hung man.

donkey lick To defeat easily.

donkey's years A long time, e.g. 'I haven't seen her for donkey's years'.

donnybrook A fight, brawl or argument.

don't come the raw prawn Used to address someone who you think is trying to deceive you, with a 'prawn' being a fool and a 'raw prawn' being a naïve fool.

don't pick your nose or your head will cave in Used to make fun of another's lack of intelligence or stupid mistake, indicating that the person's head is full of nasal mucus only, not brains.

doodad A device or gadget the name of which is forgotten.

doodle 1. To draw with no real purpose. 2. The penis.

doof or **doof-doof** Dance music, usually played loudly in a car. Comes from the sound of the thumping bass.

dook A hand. To **dook it out** is to fight in order to resolve a dispute. **Put up your dooks** is a signal to begin a fight.

do over To assault or beat up someone.

dooverlackie or **doover** A device or gadget the name of which is forgotten. Also **thingummyjig**.

dope 1. Marijuana. 2. Information, e.g. 'I've got the dope on that'. 3. A stupid person.

do-ray-me Money. An extrapolated form of 'dough', meaning money.

dork A dag or nerd. **Dorky** is that which befits a dork.

Dorothy Dixer A pre-arranged question asked of someone who knows the answer or can give a reply full of propaganda. Usually reserved for parliament but also used on other occasions. From Dorothy Dix, the pseudonym of E.M. Gilmer, the US writer of an advice column which ran from the 1890s to 1950.

dorry A gossip.

doss To sleep at a place other than one's home.

doss house A cheap house for lodging.

dot ball A ball in cricket from which no score is gained.

do the bolt To run away from something or abscond.

do the deed To have sexual intercourse.

do the Harold Holt or **do the Harry**. To run away or leave in a hurry. Rhyming slang for bolt and also refers to Prime Minister Holt who disappeared while swimming at a Victorian beach in 1967.

double To convey a second person on a bicycle, motorcycle or horse.

double adaptor A male who both gives and receives anal sex.

Double Bay tractor Sydney slang for a city-only four-wheel-drive that never sees off-road driving. Also a **Double Bay shopping trolley**.

Double Pay The affluent Sydney suburb of Double Bay.

double pluggers Thongs with two plugs keeping the straps attached to the base.

dough Money.

doughnuts Doing burnouts in a circle.

doughy Dimwitted or slow.

downer 1. A depressing occurrence. 2. A depressant drug.

down a few To have a few drinks, especially beer.

down the gurgler This is where something that is ruined or has failed goes.

Down Under Australia.

do your lolly To lose your temper.

drack Unpleasant or unattractive.

drag the chain To lag behind.

drag up or **drag up by the hair** To raise someone up in a rough way.

drain the dragon or **drain the lizard** The act of male urination. Also **syphon the python**.

drama queen A person who regularly over-reacts to minor problems.

draw the crabs To attract unwanted attention.

draw the crow To get the worst job.

dreaded lurgy A cold or a germ.

dream on An exclamation indicating something is unrealistic.

drinkies A social gathering, usually after work, for the purpose of sharing a few drinks.

drink with the flies To drink alone when at a pub.

drinky poo An alcoholic drink.

drip Describes someone who is generally dull, pathetic or colourless with little personality.

drive the porcelain bus To vomit into a toilet bowl.

drongo A dim-witted, slow person or fool.

droob The Aussie version of a nerd.

drool value Someone's perceived level of sexiness.

droolworthy or **droolsome** Spunky or luscious.

droopy drawers A slovenly, unkempt person.

drop 1. To knock someone to the ground or floor is to drop them. 2. An attractive young woman. 3. The fall of a wicket in cricket. 4. To give birth. 5. To let out a fart.

drop a bombshell To make a startling announcement.

drop a bumshell To fart.

drop bear A fictional breed of koala that supposedly leaps out of trees onto unsuspecting tourists. A tale told to frighten away tourists.

drop-in A place visited casually.

drop kick A useless or contemptible person.

drop off the twig To die.

dropsy A supposed disease in which the afflicted person often drops things.

drop test An attempt to fix a faulty item by dropping it.

drop the kids off at the pool To go to the toilet to do 'number twos'.

drop your bundle When someone loses control of a situation and gives up.

to **drop your guts** or **drop your lunch** To pass wind or fart.

drover Someone who herds or moves cattle.

drover's dog 1. Someone of no importance or who is insignificant. 2. A skinny or emaciated person is said to be **all prick and ribs like a drover's dog**.

drown some worms To go fishing.

drum 1. Good, reliable information. To **give someone the drum** is to give them some good advice or a tip. If a horse **runs a drum**, then it performs as tipped and wins. 2. A swag, so called because of its shape. To **hump the drum** was to carry a swag on the track seeking work.

drunk as a lord To be very drunk. Other phrases used are **drunk as a skunk**, **drunk as a pissant**, **drunk as a tick**, **drunk as Larry Dooley** and **drunk as Chloe**.

dry as a dead dingo's donger Very dry or extremely thirsty, donger meaning the penis. Other terms used include **dry as a frog's tit in the middle of the desert**, **dry as a bark hut**, **dry as a Pommy's bath towel**, **dry as a nun's tit** and **dry as a bark hut**.

dry rots Rhyming slang for the 'trots' or diarrhoea.

dubbo A euphemism to describe a no-hoper, a drongo, imbecile or a nerd.

dubs The toilet.

duck A score of zero runs in cricket. It is short for a duck's egg which resembles an 0. Worse still is a **golden duck**, when the batsman is out on the first ball faced, and a **diamond duck**, when the batsman is out without facing a ball.

ducks and drakes Rhyming slang for the shakes and generally brought on by a severe bout of drinking.

ducks and geese Rhyming slang for police.

duck's dinner Drinking with nothing to eat.

duck's disease An uncomplimentary way of alluding to a short person, whose bum is a lot closer to the ground than everyone else's.

duck's guts A very good thing or the best. Also **duck's nuts**.

duckshove Evading a responsibility.

ducks on the pond Floating excrement.

duco The paintwork of a vehicle.

dud 1. A failure or a loser, e.g. 'He's a real dud'. 2. To cheat someone.

dude A bloke or a fellow. It is now also used in a positive way to describe someone who is cool.

dudette A cool young woman.

dud root A crude way of saying someone is no good in bed.

duds Generally a slang term for trousers or pants but is also used for any clothing.

duffer 1. Someone who is silly or has made a silly mistake. 2. A cattle rustler.

dumbcluck A fool or someone who is stupid.

dumb down To act dumber than one actually is.

dummy spit To have a tantrum or to lose one's temper. Also to **spit the dummy**.

dump 1. A venue that is kept in a poor state. 2. An act of defecation. 3. To end a relationship with someone is to dump them. 4. A round piece cut from the centre of a silver dollar and used as a coin in the colony of NSW in the early nineteenth century.

dumper A large wave which does not break evenly from the top but crashes violently down.

dump shit on To denigrate someone.

Dunlop overcoat A condom.

dunny Great Aussie expression for the toilet. Was once used to describe an outdoor toilet but now has more widespread use to describe any toilet. The word is used in many slang phrases. If you wish that someone's good luck would change for the worse you may say **I hope your chooks turn into emus and kick your dunny down**. If you are out of luck you may exclaim **if it was raining palaces I'd be hit on the head by the dunny door** or **if it was raining virgins I'd be locked in the dunny with a poofter**. To be **all alone like a country dunny** is to be completely alone. A highly sexed woman is said to **bang like a dunny door in a gale**. Someone who has no brains **couldn't train a choko vine to grow up a dunny wall**, while something useless is said to be **as useful as a glass door on a dunny**.

dunny budgie A blowfly.

dunny can In the time before sewers, a removable can that formed the receptacle of the toilet. The job of emptying these was done by the **dunny man** while the horse-drawn cart used by him was the **dunny cart**.

dunny paper, dunny roll or **dunny documents** Toilet paper.

dunny rat Very cunning, e.g. 'He's as cunning as a dunny rat'. Also **shithouse rat**.

durry A cigarette. Claimed to be from Bull Durham which was a brand of tobacco.

dust bunny A pile of dust found under furniture in the corner of a room.

dust devil A mini whirlwind that picks up dust and rubbish.

dutch oven Created by farting under the bed covers.

dweeb A dag or nerd.

dyke 1. Slang term for a lesbian. 2. A toilet.

dykefest An organised event for lesbians.

E

eagle shits Getting paid or pay day, e.g.'Today the eagle shits'. Also **the eagle has landed**.

earbash 1. To be nagged. 2. To talk non-stop to someone.

earbasher Someone who never stops talking.

earhole The ear, e.g.'I gave him a swift hit across the earhole'.

ears flapping Listening with great interest or eavesdropping.

Eastern Suburbs Holden A Sydney slang term for a Mercedes Benz.

easy as falling off a log Very simple. Also **easy as pie** or **easy-peasy**.

easybeat A person or team who is easily beaten.

easy mark Someone who is easily conned.

easy-peasy Something that is very easy to achieve. Also used as **easy-peasy Japanesey** and **easy-peasy lemon squeezy**.

easy touch Someone who readily lends money or does other favours without thinking.

eat a horse To be very hungry and often used in the phrase **I'm so hungry I could eat a horse**.

eat dirt To lose in a race. To **eat someone's dirt** is to lose to them.

eat for breakfast To defeat someone easily in a contest, e.g.'I'll eat him for breakfast'.

eating irons Utensils.

eats Another way of saying food, e.g.'What's for eats?'

eat shit An expression of abuse often used when beating a competitor.

eau de cologne Rhyming slang for telephone.

Edgar Britt Rhyming slang for shit. To have the **Edgar Britts** is to be in a bad mood or to have diarrhoea. Often shortened to **Edgar**. Another version is **Jimmy Britts**.

effing A euphemism for fucking, e.g.'Serves him effing right'.

egg To pass wind or fart.

egg beater A helicopter.

egg flip Rhyming slang for tip, as at the races.

egghead 1. A fool or idiot. 2. An intellectual or highbrow person.

egg roll An idiot.

eggshell blonde A bald person.

eh A word used at the end of a sentence, generally as a form of question. In

Queensland the term is often used at the end of nearly every sentence, eh.

eighteen An 18-gallon beer keg.

the **Ekka** 1. The Royal Queensland Show. 2. The Brisbane Exhibition Showground.

elastics A girl's schoolyard game.

elastic sides Boots with a piece of elastic set into the sides.

el cheapo Something that is cheap and inferior.

elbow grease Vigorous hard work, e.g. 'Put some elbow grease into it'.

elephant bucks A large amount of money.

elephant gun A surfboard used to ride big waves.

elephant juice 1. A narcotic used to immobilise large animals but now used in small amounts to illegally stimulate racehorses. 2. A rough, powerful alcoholic drink.

elephant's trunk Rhyming slang for drunk and often shortened to **elephants**.

your **elevator doesn't go to the top floor** A derogatory term for someone considered stupid.

Elvis Presley 1. A term used by car salesmen to describe a car with many dents and scratches in the duco, in reference to it having had many hits. 2. Among fishermen, a leatherjacket fish.

Emerald City A nickname for Sydney, equal to the home of the Wizard of Oz.

Emma Chisit 'How much is it' as spoken in 'Strine'.

emo Short for emotional.

empties Empty beer bottles.

emu-bob To bend down and pick up things in order to clear an area. An **emu-bobber** is someone who does this.

emu parade Any group of people collecting litter or unwanted material from an area. It was originally a military parade to clean up an area but is now used for any such group, particularly school children. The term is also used to describe a line of police combing an area for forensic evidence. Also called an **emu bob**, **emu patrol**, **emu walk** or **emu stalk**.

Enzed A shortened term for New Zealand. **Enzedder** is a New Zealander.

erky Revolting. Also **erky perky**.

eskimo pie An ice-cream wafer.

Esky An insulated, portable container traditionally used to keep beer cool. It is a brand name but is now used to describe any such container.

esky lid A derogatory term used by surfies to describe a bodyboard.

euchre or **euchred** To outwit someone.

even stevens To be equal or on a level playing field.

every Tom Dick and Harry or **every bastard and his dog** The general public or a big crowd.

everything that opens and shuts All possible embellishments or decorations.

the **evil weed** Marijuana.

evo Shortened version of evening.

exec An executive.

exo Excellent. A term often used by teenagers.

ex-pug A retired boxer.

extracurricular Sexual activities outside a relationship.

exy Shortened form of expensive.

eyeball To look at something or someone.

Eyetie Derogatory term for an Italian. Also **Itie.**

F

fabbo An Australian way of saying fab or fabulous.

face ache An ugly or irritating person.

face fungus Any hair on the face, such as a beard or moustache.

face like a ... Someone with an ugly face is said to have **a face like a smashed crab**. Other examples include **face like the northbound end of a southbound cow**, **face like a dropped pie** and **face like a half eaten pastie**.

face like a festered pickle A description of someone who is suffering from acne.

face plant A heavy fall from a skateboard, snowboard or skis.

fag 1. Slang expression for a cigarette. 2. A euphemism for a homosexual man.

faggot A derogatory term for a homosexual man.

fag hag A woman who socialises with male homosexuals.

fair Absolute or complete.

fair cop Just punishment or outcome.

fair cow Something that is distinctly unpleasant.

fair crack of the whip An exclamation used when asking to be given a fair chance.

fair dinkum 1. Genuine, true or correct. 2. Typical Australian honesty, guts and determination.

fair enough All right, fair or no worries.

fair go A fair or reasonable opportunity. Giving people a fair go is a traditional aspect of the national character.

fair suck of the sav Give me a fair go. Also **fair suck of the sauce bottle**, **fair suck of the Siberian sandshoe** or just **fair suck**.

fairy 1. A derogatory term for an effeminate male homosexual. To be **full as a fairy's phonebook** is to be completely full of food or booze. 2. The fluffy airborne seed of various plants.

fairy floss The Australian name for the pink spun sugar often obtained at fetes and shows. The English call it candy floss and the Yanks call it cotton candy.

falcon Being hit in the head with the ball in rugby league.

family jewels The testicles.

fang 1. To borrow something. If you fang someone for a couple of bucks, you have just borrowed a couple of dollars. 2. A tooth. To **go the fang** or to **fang down** is to tuck into food and to be **good on the fang** is to be a hearty eater.

fang artist A voracious eater.

fang carpenter A dentist.

fang it To drive fast or put the foot down on the accelerator.

fanny Slang term for the female genitalia. In the US this is used to refer to the buttocks.

fanny tickler A small tuft of facial hair under the bottom lip on an otherwise clean-shaven face.

fantabulous Marvellous or wonderful.

fark A representation of the Australian pronunciation of fuck, popularised by TV personality Graham Kennedy.

Farmer Giles Rhyming slang for piles or haemorrhoids.

far out Amazing or incredible.

fart 1. To pass wind. In rhyming slang it is known as a **Royce Hart**. 2. Old people are often referred to as **old farts**. 3. If you are very drunk you might be described as **full as a fart** or **pissed as a fart**.

fart a crowbar An expression of annoyance.

fart arse A contemptible person.

fart-arsing Wasting time, e.g. 'I wish he'd stop fart-arsing around'.

fart face A mild insult directed at someone who is proving annoying.

fart fodder Baked beans.

farts like a two-stroke Someone with a noisy flatulence problem.

fartmobile A car with a muffler that produces a fart-like sound.

fart sack Sleeping bag.

fart sparks Venting anger, similar to 'spitting chips'.

fat 1. An erect penis. 2. A fattened cow or bull that is ready for market. 3. Excellent or cool.

fat chance Little hope of doing something.

fat day A day on which someone feels fatter than normal.

fat farm A resort where people go to lose weight.

a **fat lot** Very little, e.g. 'That will do a fat lot of good'.

fatty-boom-bah A taunting nickname for a fat person. Also **fatty boombuster**, **fatty-boom-sticks** or **fatty-boom-bah-sticks**.

fave Favourite.

faze To disturb or daunt someone.

fed A federal police officer or any police officer.

feeding time at the zoo Description of the rabble often found when there is something free or cheap on offer.

feed the fishes To be seasick.

feel crook To feel unwell.

feisty High spirited and volatile.

fella A man.

it **fell off the back of a truck** A way of describing something obtained by questionable or illegal means.

feminazi A derogatory name for an extreme feminist.

femmo A feminist.

feral 1. A bogan. 2. Disgusting or gross and often used to describe people who are gross. 3. A hippie environmentalist. 4. Unrestrained or wild.

ferret 1. A cricket player at the end of the batting order. 2. The penis. Used in phrases such as **give the ferret a run**, **exercise the ferret** and **run the ferret up the drainpipe**.

fess up To confess to something.

fester To waste time while you are meant to be studying.

fetch Used by young people to indicate that something or someone is cool.

a **few** To have a few beers.

a **few sardines short of a tin** Not having full intelligence. Also a **few snags short of a barbie**.

fibber Someone who tells lies.

fibro 1. Abbreviation of fibrocement, which for many years was the basic component of domestic architecture in Australia. 2. A fibro is someone who lives in the suburbs dominated by fibro houses.

fiddle fart To waste time, e.g. 'Don't fiddle fart around'.

field To work as a bookmaker. A **fielder** is a bookmaker.

fifty-fifty 1. A glass of beer that is half filled with old and half with new. 2. A dance at which the music is half old-time and half modern.

figjam A conceited person — an acronym from 'Fuck I'm Good, Just Ask Me'.

fillum The Aussie way of saying the word 'film'.

filly A term for a sexy young woman.

filth 1. Excellent, brilliant. A word often used by young people. 2. The police.

filthy 1. Angry or enraged. 2. Very good or excellent.

finer than frog's hair Something that is very fine.

finger 1. To accuse someone. 2. To **pull your finger out** is to get down to business after being inactive. 3. To **give someone the finger** is to make an obscene gesture.

finger stalls The back row seats of a cinema where you can get away with doing things that you couldn't do if you were sitting elsewhere.

fire To go well.

fire away To begin doing something or begin speaking.

firie Abbreviation of firefighter.

firing blanks Experiencing orgasm but not ejaculating or doing so with infertile sperm.

first beer won't touch the sides An expression said by someone who is very thirsty and hanging out for a beer.

first cab off the rank The first person to do something.

fisho 1. A fisherman. 2. A fish and chip shop.

fish out of water Describes someone who feels uncomfortable doing something.

fit 1. To convict an innocent person, also to **fit up**. 2. Equipment used to prepare and inject drugs.

fit as a mallee bull Very fit and healthy person.

fits like a honeymoon cock A very neat fit.

five-dog night A bitterly cold night in the bush. About the coldest night you can get.

five finger discount Shoplifting.

five o'clock shadow The growth of stubble on a man's face.

fiver A $5 note.

fix A shot of heroin or some other drug.

fizzer 1. A dud firecracker. 2. A failure or dud.

fizzy drink Carbonated soft drink.

flab Fat.

flake Shark meat, often used in fish and chip shops when you simply ask for fish rather than specifying a particular species.

flake out To lie down, to sleep or to collapse.

flaming A favourite Australian adjective often used instead of saying 'fuck'. Can be used to add emphasis to something, e.g. 'We had a flaming good time'.

flaming fury A toilet constructed over a pit, the contents of which are doused with oil and burnt.

flannie A flannelette shirt. Also a **flanno.**

flap 1. A blank cheque leaf. 2. If someone says **get your flaps off me** it means they want to be left alone.

flap your gums To talk a lot.

flash Showy.

flash a brown eye To expose one's bottom.

flash as a rat with a gold tooth Extremely showy.

flat The centre area of a racecourse.

flatfoot A police officer.

flat chat or **flat out** To go as fast as possible.

flat out like a lizard drinking. To be very busy doing something.

flattie 1. Ladies shoes with low heels. 2. A flatmate or roommate. 3. A flat-bottomed boat.

flea bag An animal infested with fleas or a shabby-looking person.

flea pit A shabby room or building.

fleas and itches Rhyming slang for the pictures or the cinema.

flick To get rid of something or somebody, e.g. 'She's given me the flick'.

flicks Slang term for the movies or a picture theatre.

flied lice A pronunciation of fried rice that mocks the Chinese.

flip 1. A silly person. 2. To become angry, also **flip out** or **flip your lid**.

flip flops Rubber thongs.

flipping Often used instead of the four letter F word.

floater 1. Excrement floating in a toilet. 2. In the game of two-up, a coin that fails to spin when thrown in the air. 3. A dead person found floating in the water.

flog 1. To sell something. 2. To use something a lot.

flog the lizard To masturbate.

flooze To flirt openly or to sleep around.

floozy A derogatory term for a promiscuous woman.

fluff 1. A quaint Aussie term for breaking wind. 2. A description of a good-looking woman, e.g. 'That's a nice bit of fluff. 3. To make a blunder.

fluke A lucky break that happens purely by chance.

flute The penis.

flutter A bet.

flutter-by A spoonerism of butterfly

fly 1. To attempt something. 2. Awake to something. 3. Cool and stylish. In this manner the word is used by many young people.

flyblown 1. To be drunk. 2. Broke or penniless.

flybog Jam, because it bogs flies if they land in it.

fly cemetery or **fly sandwich** A biscuit with dried fruit between two layers of sweet biscuit.

flyer 1. A fast kangaroo. 2. A fast train service. 3. A fast shearer.

flying axe handles Describes having diarrhoea.

flying cane toad A disparaging name for the Indian myna bird which was introduced into Australia in the 1860s and is now a common pest in large cities and cane-growing areas.

the **Flying Doormat** A nickname for 1970s Aussie Rules player Bruce Doull.

flying fox Rhyming slang for pox.

the **Flying Peanut** A nickname bestowed upon former Queensland premier Sir Joh Bjelke-Petersen who was an aviator and peanut farmer.

fly's eyes A childish male display of the testicles carried out by placing each one out through the leg hole of underwear.

fly the coop To leave home.

folding stuff Bank notes.

folkie A folk music fan or performer.

folks Your parents or relatives.

follicularly challenged Bald or going bald.

foodie A food connoisseur.

foof To expand in all directions at the one time, or fluffy.

footbrawl A derogatory name for football codes other than the one the speaker follows.

foot falcon The feet when used as a form of transport. Particularly used in northern Australia. Also **Shanks's pony**.

Footscray florsheims Melbourne slang for ugg boots or slippers.

footsy A childish name for a foot. To **play footsies** is to touch someone else's feet under a table.

footy 1. An Australian description of any code of football but particularly used for the code most popular in a particular state. 2. A football.

footy nicks The short shorts worn by Aussie Rules players.

Forest Fortnight Another name for Bush Week and usually used in the reply 'What do you think it is, Bush Week? No, Forest Fortnight'.

fork out To pay one's debt or to pay for anything.

fork over To hand something over.

form 1. Someone's luck. 2. A person's character.

for openers To begin with or to start. Also **for starters**.

fossil An old person or thing.

foulie To be in a bad or foul mood.

fourby 1. A piece of four-by-two timber. 2. A four-wheel-drive.

four-by-two 1. Rhyming slang for 'screw' or a prison warden. 2. Rhyming slang for Jew.

four-dog-night A cold night in the bush.

four-eyes A person who wears spectacles.

four-legged lottery Any horse race.

fourpenny dark Cheap red wine.

four pointer 1. A try in rugby league. 2. Two slices of bread with filling, cut diagonally.

fox To fetch or to get.

foxie A fox terrier dog.

frang A sausage.

franger Slang term for a condom.

freaking A euphemism for the word fucking.

freckle 1. The anus. 2. A chocolate lolly with hundreds and thousands on top.

fred An annoying electrical device. An acronym from Fucking Ridiculous Electronic Device.

Fred Astaire 1. Rhyming slang for chair. 2. Rhyming slang for hair.

Fred Nerk An imaginary person generally considered to be the archetypal Aussie drongo or nerd.

freeballing or **free snake it** Wearing no underpants.

the **Freezer** The Antarctic.

freeze your tits off To be very cold.

freight Euphemism for money.

Fremantle doctor A strong southerly wind which blows through Fremantle and Perth late on hot summer days.

French A humorous term for swear words, e.g. 'Please excuse my French'.

French cut In cricket a ball that is edged wide of leg stump.

French tickler A condom with an attachment on the end to give extra stimulation.

Frenchy A condom.

Freo The city of Fremantle, WA.

freshie A freshwater crocodile.

fricking A euphemism for the word fucking.

fridge Common term for refrigerator.

fried egg A traffic dome, also known as a **silent cop**.

frig 1. To masturbate. 2. To have sexual intercourse. 3. An exclamation of surprise or shock and used as an alternative to fuck.

frig about To waste time.

frigging A euphemism for the word fucking.

frigging in the rigging Wasting time.

frigid digit A sexually unresponsive penis.

frig up To wreck or damage something.

frillie A frill-necked lizard.

frog 1. A derogatory term for a French person. 2. A condom.

frog and toad Rhyming slang for road.

from away Anyone not from the local area is 'from away'.

from go to whoa From start to finish. Also **from arsehole to breakfast time**.

front Brash, bold and totally unashamed.

frosty An ice-cold beer.

froth and bubble 1. Rhyming slang for trouble. 2. Rhyming slang for a double at the racetrack.

frozen mitt A slang term for the 'cold shoulder'.

fruit and veg The male genitalia.

fruitcake A nut case or a ratbag.

fruit loop Someone who is considered crazy or loopy.

fruit salad Military slang for a large collection of medal ribbons.

fruity 1. Crazy, insane or weird. 2. In SA, an hysterical fit.

fuck The quintessential Australian four-letter word with many different meanings. It has lost some of its impact in recent years due to common use and is now allowed on public television after 9.30 p.m. 1. To have sexual intercourse. 2. The act of sexual intercourse. 3. To ruin or spoil something is **to fuck it up**. 4. A contemptible person. 5. A word of abuse having more impact or emphasis than 'damn'. 6. An exclamation used to express annoyance such as when you hit your finger with a hammer, or even amazement or delight. 7. **Not to give a flying fuck** is not to care at all. 8. A man desperate for sexual intercourse **would fuck a hole in the ground if it smiled at him**.

fuckable Sexually desirable.

fuck about or **fuck around** To waste time. To fuck someone about is to treat them unfairly.

fuck a duck! Wow.

fuck all Very little. Also **fuck all in Blackall**.

fucked 1. Broken or wrecked. 2. In an impossible situation. 3. Exhausted. 4. Astounded. 5. Bothered. 6. Drunk or stoned. 7. Extremely bad.

fucked by the fickle finger of fate Suffering bad fortune.

fucked if I know Ignorance or not knowing the answer to a question.

fucked in the head Insane or crazy.

fucked up 1. Emotionally wrecked. 2. Completely bad. 3. A mistake. Also **fuck-up.**

fucker 1. A contemptible person. 2. Any person or anything.

fuckface A contemptible person.

fucking 1. Sexual intercourse. 2. Contemptible. Usually used as an intensifier.

fucking well Absolutely. Used as an intensifier.

fuck-knuckle An idiot or a wanker.

fuck-load A lot.

fuck me, I'll be damned An exclamation of surprise. Also **fuck me dead**, **fuck me blind** or **fuck me drunk.**

fuck off 1. An expression of rejection or a command. 2. To depart. 3. Disbelief. 4. To annoy.

fucks me It beats me, or I don't know.

fuck up To blunder or to make a mistake.

fuck wit A stupid person or someone who doesn't think before they do something.

fuck with To meddle with.

fuck you Damn you.

fudge packer A homosexual male.

fugly Unattractive, a combination of fucking and ugly.

full Intoxicated, overcrowded or unable to eat any more. Also **full as a boot**, **full as a goog**, **full as a bull**, **a bull's bum**, **a butcher's pup**, **an egg**, **a Catholic school**, **a State school**, **hat rack**, **a fart**, **a tick**, **a Corby boogie board bag**, **a fairy's phone book**, **a Pommy complaint box**, **a fat lady's sock**, **bra**, **undies** or **gumboot**, or a **seaside shithouse on Boxing Day**. Also **full up to dolly's wax** or **full up to pussy's bow**.

full bore To the maximum.

full bottle An expert.

full of beans An energetic person.

full of it Someone who is talking nonsense is said to be this. Also **full of shit**.

full of yourself Conceited.

full on Intense or confronting.

fully sick Really good.

fun bags Breasts.

fungus face A person with a beard or other facial hair.

funny farm A psychiatric hospital.

funny money Money made by dubious means.

furburger The female genitalia.

furniture The stumps in a game of cricket.

furphy A lie or a rumour.

Fuzzy Wuzzy Angels A term used to describe the native Papua New Guineans who helped the Australian soldiers during World War II.

the **F-word** A euphemism for the word fuck.

G

gab To chatter or talk incessantly.

the **Gabba** Shortened name of the Woolloongabba Cricket Ground in Brisbane.

ga-ga To become besotted by something or someone.

gagging for To be desirous of someone or something.

galah A silly person or a loud, rudely behaved person.

galah session A time when the people of isolated outback areas converse with one another by radio.

galoot An awkward or silly person, also a drip or a drongo.

galvo Abbreviation of galvanised iron.

game 1. A business or profession, e.g. 'Mike's in the building game'. To be **on the game** is to be in the business of prostitution. 2. Plucky or courageous. 3. To **give the game away** is to stop or abandon what you are doing or your profession.

game as a pissant To be very daring.

game as Ned Kelly Adventurous or foolhardy. To be imbued with the same fighting spirit as bushranger Ned Kelly. Also **game as Phar Lap** in reference to Australia's national horseracing hero of the 1930s.

gammon To lie or fib.

gander Have a look at something.

gangbusters If something is going really well it is said to be **going gangbusters**.

gank Stealing or shoplifting.

garage door The fly. If someone's garage door is open, their trouser fly is undone.

garbage bird The pesky Indian myna bird.

garbage guts Someone who will eat anything or someone who eats too much.

garbo A garbage collector or a garbage bin.

garbologist A garbage collector.

gargle An alcoholic drink, e.g. 'Would you like a gargle?'

gasbag Someone who talks a lot.

gas guzzler A car that uses a lot of fuel.

gasper A cigarette.

gastro Abbreviation of gastroenteritis. Used to describe any type of stomach bug or ailment.

Gawler Place Adelaide rhyming slang for face.

gawk To have a good look at someone or something, or to stare.

gay 1. Homosexual. Originally and still mainly used to describe men but it now is also used to refer to lesbians. 2. Among young people it means uncool or daggy.

gay and hearty Rhyming slang for a party.

gazunder A potty that 'gazunder' (goes under) the bed. Now also used to describe any toilet.

G-banger A G-string that shows above the pants. Also known as a **whale's tail.**

g'day Ubiquitous Australian way of saying good day.

gear 1. Your clothes. 2. An illegal drug. 3. Apparatus used to prepare and inject drugs. 4. Used to refer to whatever is being discussed.

gee $1000. Taken from 'g' as in a 'grand'.

the **Gee** A commonly used nickname for the Melbourne Cricket Ground.

gee-gee Childish expression for a horse.

geek 1. To have a look is to have a geek at something. 2. A nerd or any person who is not cool. In schools this term is used to describe a conscientious student. Also **geeky.**

geek boy or **geek guy** A male computer enthusiast. **Geek girl** or **geek chick** is the female equivalent.

geekspeak Jargon used by computer geeks.

geekster A computer geek.

gee up To stir up or to excite someone.

geez 1. Strike me pink or holy cow. In this form it is an euphemistic abbreviation of Jesus. 2. When pronounced with a hard 'g' it means to look at.

geezer 1. A funny old man. 2. A look.

gen General information.

gen up To read up on something.

geo A geologist.

geri Short for geriatric or old.

Germaine Greer Rhyming slang for beer.

gestapo Melbourne slang for ticket inspectors. Also used more widely in reference to any authorities.

get a black dog up you Get stuffed.

get a guernsey To get a start in any sporting team.

get a leg over To have sexual intercourse.

get a life Don't be so hopeless and do something worthwhile.

get a load of To have a look at something or study it.

get amongst it To get involved in something.

get a wriggle on Hurry up.

get it off To have sex.

get it up 1. To scold or abuse someone. 2. To achieve an erection.

get nicked Exclamation of contempt. Also **get knotted**.

get off at Redfern To pull out of sexual intercourse before ejaculation. Redfern is the final stop before Central Railway Station, the hub of Sydney's rail system.

get off on 1. To be excited about something. 2. To be sexually stimulated.

get on To place a bet.

get on your goat To be really annoyed.

get some pork on your fork Of a male, to obtain sexual intercourse.

get stuffed A term of abuse. Also **get rooted** or **get fucked**.

gettas Thongs.

get the axe To be dismissed for work. Also **get the chop** or **get the sack**.

get the money To win on a horse race or a bet.

get the shits up To get upset.

getting any? A short way of asking 'Are you getting any sexual intercourse?'

get up 1. To win, e.g. 'The greyhound managed to get up in the last stride'. 2. To annoy someone greatly.

get your arse into gear Get ready for action, hurry up or get busy.

get your end in To obtain sexual intercourse.

get your flaps off me Leave me alone.

get your rocks off 1. To enjoy something immensely. 2. To orgasm.

get your wick wet 1. Of a male, to have sexual intercourse. 2. Of a male to lose his virginity.

the **GG** The Governor-General.

Ghan 1. A train on the Adelaide to Darwin route. 2. An Afghan camel driver in outback Australia.

gibber A small stone suitable for throwing. A region covered with gibbers in the arid Australian outback is called a **gibber plain**, **gibber desert** or **gibber country**.

gig 1. A performance event, e.g. 'She's got a gig tonight'. 2. A fool. 3. To kid or tease someone. 4. A look. 5. A police informer.

giggle house A psychiatric hospital or institution. Also a **giggle factory**.

giggle suit Army greens.

gilgie A type of freshwater crayfish in WA, related to the yabby.

gilgie's piss In WA, a term for poor-tasting beer.

gimp 1. A fool or an idiot. 2. To pay out on someone.

gin A racist name for an Aboriginal woman.

ginger The backside, e.g. 'I gave him a swift kick up the ginger'. This word is from **ginger ale**, which is rhyming slang for tail. If someone is **on your ginger** they are chasing you or right behind you.

ginger beer Rhyming slang for engineer.

gin jockey Racist term for a white male who has sexual relations with an Aboriginal woman.

gink A guy or a fellow.

gin's handbag A cask of wine.

gin's piss Horrible beer.

gin sling Rhyming slang for ring as in a telephone call.

girlie 1. A girl or young woman. 2. A disparaging term for effeminate things that should be masculine. 3. Used to refer to naked photos of women, as in **girlie magazines**.

girl's blouse An ineffectual, timid male. Also **big girl's blouse**.

girls' night out An evening occasion involving only women.

give a gobful To tell someone the truth.

give a shit To care or appreciate. Often used as a negative, e.g. 'I don't really give a shit'.

give birth to a politician To defecate.

give it a burl To have a go at something, e.g. 'All right. I'll give it a burl'.

give it away To give up on.

give lip To be cheeky.

give the game away To abandon what you are doing.

gladdies Abbreviation of gladioli.

glad rags Good clothes or 'Sunday best'.

glamour A good-looking woman.

glass can A beer stubbie.

glum bum A pessimist.

go 1. To attempt something, e.g. 'Give it here, I'll have a go'. This has led to the great Aussie cry 'Have a go, ya mug'. 2. A fight. 3. An opportunity to be taken. 4. Eating or drinking with pleasure, e.g. 'I could really go a beer'.

go all the way To have sexual intercourse.

goal sneak A player who catches the opposition unawares in Aussie Rules and scores a goal.

goanna Rhyming slang for 'pianner', or piano.

go ape shit To become very angry.

goat 1. A fool. 2. A lecherous old man. 3. A racehorse that is no good. If it **runs like a hairy goat** then it won't be winning. 4. If something **gets (on) your goat** then it annoys you.

gob 1. Slang term for the mouth. 2. To gobble something down. 3. To spit.

gobsmacked Astonished at something.

go bung To cease to operate properly.

go crook To tell someone off or to get angry.

God Nickname of Aussie Rules legend Gary Ablett.

go down the tubes To fail.

God's gift to ... A wonderful person in their sphere of interest. Also often used in a sarcastic or derogatory sense to mean the opposite.

God squad A group or gathering of Christian people.

goer 1. An energetic person who never stops doing things. 2. A project having good prospects of success, as in 'It's a goer'.

go for the doctor 1. To go all out. 2. To bet all your money on a horse. 3. In horseracing it is the time when the jockey gets the whip out.

go gangbusters To go along well or perform well. Also to **go great guns**.

goggles Glasses or spectacles.

gold-digger Someone who marries for financial gain.

golden arches A McDonald's family restaurant.

golden drinking token or **GDT** A $50 note.

golden duck A first ball dismissal in cricket.

the **Golden Mile** A gold-rich reef between Kalgoorlie and Boulder in WA.

goldfish bowl Any room with a large window at street level or a room with walls of glass in an office environment.

Goldsborough Morts Rhyming slang for shorts.

go like a shower of shit To go very fast.

go like the clappers To go very fast.

golly Saliva and mucus collected in the mouth and spat out. Also called a **gooby** or a **gorby**.

gone 1. Ruined or wrecked. 2. Pregnant.

gone a million Completely undone.

goner Someone who is beyond help or dead, e.g. 'I'm afraid he's a goner'.

gone like last week's pay Nothing left.

Gone to Gowings NSW slang for departing in great haste. Can also mean destitute, drunk, hung over, losing a race or a game and insane. This is taken from an advertising campaign for the former Sydney menswear store Gowings, in which someone made a hasty departure saying they had 'Gone to Gowings'.

gone to the dogs Describes something that has changed from good to bad.

gong A medal or award.

the **Gong** The NSW city of Wollongong.

goober A stupid or annoying person.

good as gold Something that is very good.

goodbye muscles The flabby triceps of an overweight or matronly female.

good call A good decision.

good looker An attractive person.

good nick Something that is in good condition.

good oh An Australian way of saying very good or okay.

good oil Reliable information. Also just **the oil**.

good on ya mate! Well done. A positive exclamation. Also **good onya** or just **onya**.

good sort An attractive woman.

good thing A tip for a racehorse.

good trot A run of good luck.

good wicket To be in a position of advantage.

goof A clumsy fool. To **goof up** is to make a mistake. To **goof off** is to loaf and to **goof around** is to play the fool.

go off 1. To be thrilling, e.g. 'The dancers were really going off'. 2. To vent anger loudly. 3. To be raided or arrested by police.

go off like a frog in a sock To really go off.

goofy 1. Silly or clumsy. 2. A left-footed surfer, skater or snowboarder. Also **goofy foot**, **goofy footed** or **goofy footer**.

googie An egg. Also **goog** or **googie egg**.

goon A flagon of wine or cheap cask wine.

goon bag The silver bladder inside a wine cask.

goon box A cask of cheap wine.

goose 1. Someone who is a bit silly or does something silly. 2. Something you do to someone when you sneak up behind them and grab them between the buttocks.

goose juice Alcohol or booze.

goose's neck Rhyming slang for a cheque.

gormless Slow and stupid.

Gosford dog Rhyming slang for a wog, or person of Mediterranean background.

Gosford skirt A very short skirt. So called because the NSW city of Gosford is close to The Entrance. Also **Gosford boots** for knee-high boots.

gospel Truth, the absolute truth.

goss 1. Gossip. 2. The latest news, e.g. 'Give me the goss'.

go to buggery Get lost or go away.

got out quicker than rats deserting a sinking ship To leave or depart quickly.

go the knuckle To fight someone with the fists.

go the whole hog To go all the way.

go through To leave or abscond.

go to the pack or **gone to the pack** To deteriorate.

go walkabout Wandering off or go missing, e.g. 'Jimmy has gone walkabout'.

go walkies To set out on a journey.

grab A mark in Aussie Rules.

grab by the balls To impress or to make someone take notice.

grab forty winks To have a short nap.

graft Hard work. A hard worker is a **grafter**.

Granny An affectionate name for the *Sydney Morning Herald* newspaper.

grape cocky A winegrower.

grape on the business An unwelcome person, a wallflower or a drag on cheery company. First recorded in 1941, origin unknown.

grass 1. Marijuana. 2. To inform on or dob in a colleague. Also **grass up**. **Grasser** is an informer.

grass castle A mansion paid for from the proceeds of marijuana.

grasshopper Derogatory term for a tourist.

gravel rash What you get from crawling to the boss or authorities.

graveyard chompers False teeth.

greaser A crawler or sycophant.

greasies Fish and chips.

greasy 1. Racist term for a Greek, Italian or someone from the Mediterranean area. 2. A shearer. 3. A disapproving look, short for **greasy eyeball**.

greasy spoon A cheap and nasty hamburger shop or takeaway joint.

great Australian adjective The word 'bloody'.

great galloping goannas An expression of amazement.

the **Great South Land** Australia.

greeblies Germs.

green and gold Australia's international sporting colours. Proclaimed the national colours in 1984.

green around the gills Feeling ill or sick.

green can A can of Victoria Bitter beer.

green death Victoria Bitter beer as described by those who dislike it. Also used disparagingly for Southwark beer in SA.

green giant A plastic $100 note.

greenie 1. Slang term for an environmentalist. 2. A lump of mucus ejected or picked from the nose.

Gregory Peck Rhyming slang for a cheque, often shortened to **Gregory**. Also rhyming slang for neck.

grenade A small bottle of beer. Also called a **throwdown**, **twist top** or **twistie**.

grey A grey kangaroo.

grey ghost A parking inspector in NSW, Victoria and SA. Also called **grey meanies** or **brown bombers**.

grey nomad An older person, often retired, who travels around the country in a caravan or motorhome.

grey nurse An old paper $100 note.

grid A bicycle.

grinning like a shot fox To be smugly satisfied or very happy.

grizzle To complain constantly. Someone who complains a lot is called a **grizzleguts**.

grog 1. Alcohol or booze. 2. A glass of alcohol, e.g. 'I'm just going to have a few grogs'.

grog bog A noisy and smelly excrement produced the morning after a night of heavy drinking.

grog on To take part in a drinking session.

grog shop A retail outlet where alcohol is sold.

grommet A young surfer but also used to describe any young person.

gronk A fool or an idiot.

groover 1. A person who is cool. 2. Someone dancing to music. Dancers are **groovers and shakers**.

grope To fondle sexually.

groper A Western Australian. A shortening of sandgroper. **Groperland** is WA.

gross Revolting or digusting.

gross out To disgust.

grot 1. A dirty or untidy person. 2. Dirt or mess. 3. To spit on someone.

grotty Dirty or filthy.

ground lice Sheep.

grouse Great, terrific.

grouter To **come in on the grouter** is to arrive after the work has been finished. Laying the grout is the last job to be done when tiling.

grub 1. Slang term for food. 2. Someone who is dirty or untidy. 3. A non-union worker who enjoys benefits provided by the union.

grumblebum A whinger.

grumpy bum Someone who is always grumpy.

grundies Rhyming slang for undies. Short for **Reg Grundies**.

grunt Power or strength.

gubba A derogatory word used by Aboriginals for a white person.

guff Silly talk.

guilts Feelings of remorse.

gully raker 1. A cattle thief who steals unbranded cattle. 2. A stockwhip. 3. A thunderstorm bringing heavy rain.

gumby 1. A fool. 2. A calf raised on the bottle. 3. In Victoria, a public transport employee.

gum digger A dentist. Also a **gum puncher.**

gummies Slang for gumboots.

gumsucker A disparaging name for a Victorian.

gum tree The Australian eucalypt. **Up a gum tree** is to be in all sorts of strife. To be **mad as a gum tree full of galahs** is to be crazy or bonkers.

gum tree mail The delivery of letters in remote areas whereby the sender places the letter in a cleft stick from a gum tree for the driver or guard from a passing train to snatch as the train goes past.

gun 1. A champion shearer. 2. To rev an engine and drive at great speed. 3. A large surfboat for riding big waves.

Gundy Shortened form of the Queensland town of Goondiwindi.

gunge 1. Filthy or messy. 2. Marijuana.

gunna or **gunner** A procrastinator. Used in the phrase 'He's a real gunna' to describe someone who is always going to (or 'gunna') do something but never does.

gunyah An Aboriginal shelter made from bark and tree boughs.

gurgler A plughole. If something has **gone down the gurgler** it has failed.

gutful 1. Short for gut full of piss. To be drunk, e.g. 'I think he's had a gutful'. 2. To have had enough of someone, e.g. 'I've had a gutful of him.'

gutless wonder A coward.

guts 1. Essential information, e.g. 'I'll get to the guts of the matter'. 2. To **drop your guts** is to fart.

a **gutzer** To fall over or fall off something. If you do this you are said to have **come a gutzer.**

guy magnet A woman who is attractive to many men.

guy-watch To ogle males.

gym junkie A person addicted to the gym.

gyp Swindle.

Gyppo An old racist term for an Egyptian. Also spelt **Gippo**.

H

hack To deal with or cope, e.g. 'I can't hack it anymore'.

had it 1. To run out of patience, e.g. 'That's it, I've had it.' 2. To cease operating, e.g. 'That old TV's had it'.

had the dick Ruined, wrecked, broken or worn out. Also **had the chad**, **had the rod**, **had the stick** and **had the Richard**.

ha-ha pigeon A kookaburra.

hair dryer A hand-held police radar unit.

hair like a bush pig's arse Unmanageable hair.

hair of the dog To have another drink when you've got a hangover after a big night out.

hairy armpit brigade A collective name for radical feminists.

hairy chequebook Sexual intercourse used by a woman as a payment.

hairy eyeball A disapproving look.

hairy goat A badly performing racehorse. If a horse runs like a hairy goat it won't be winning.

hairy leg A railway fettler. Also **snake charmer** and **woolly nose**.

half a mo' Just wait a moment.

half-inch Rhyming slang for pinch or steal.

half-pie Halfway or not fully.

half-tanked Partly drunk.

half your luck Very lucky or good on you.

ham and eggs Rhyming slang for legs.

hammer 1. Heroin. From the rhyming slang hammer and tack or smack. 2. Also rhyming slang for back. If someone is on your hammer they are following you closely. 3. To drive at speed. 4. The accelerator. 5. To be well beaten.

hammered Drunk.

hammie Hamstring, e.g. 'He's done a hammie'.

handbag An attractive male used by a woman as a showpiece when going out to social functions.

handbrake A man's wife or girlfriend seen as an obstacle to enjoyment.

handbrakie A turn made in a car by slamming on the handbrake when driving at speed.

hand grenade A small bottle of beer. Also a **throwdown**.

handle 1. A person's name. 2. A beer glass with a handle. 3. To **get a handle on** something is to comprehend it.

as **handy as an ashtray on a motorbike** Something that is useless.

hang 1. Changing course. 2. To perform a bodily function. 3. To frequent something or spend time in.

hanger A spectacular mark in Aussie Rules.

hang five 1. To ride a surfboard standing on the nose of the board with the toes of a foot over the edge. With the toes of both feet is **hang ten**. 2. Hold on a minute, e.g. 'Hang five while I go back inside'.

hanging To be eager to do something, e.g. 'I'm hanging for a beer'.

hang on a tick Wait for a minute.

hanging shit on To denigrate someone.

hang with, **hang out** or **hang around** To spend time with someone or friends.

happening Very good, cool or really going off, e.g. 'This pub is really happening'.

happy as a bastard on Father's Day Unhappy or miserable.

happy as a pig in shit To be very happy. Also **happy as a dog with two tails**.

happy as Larry To be extremely happy.

happy camper A person who is quite pleased but usually used in the negative as in 'She was not a happy camper'.

happy chappie A pleased male but often used in the negative as in 'He's not a happy chappie'.

happy juice Alcohol or any pain-relieving liquid medicine.

happy little Vegemite Describes someone in a good mood or contented.

hard case A person who does not conform to what others think, a heavy drinker or an eccentric person.

hard cheese Tough luck. Also **stiff cheese**.

hard doer Someone who does it hard.

harder to pick than a broken nose A contest that is very difficult to predict.

hard graft Hard work or hard yakka.

Hardly Normal A perversion of the department store Harvey Norman.

hard-on An erect penis.

hard stuff Hard liquor such as spirits.

it's **hard to soar like an eagle when you're dealing with turkeys** To deal with stupid people or idiots.

hard word A strong request.

hard yakka Back-breaking work.

hard yards Hard work that is necessary to achieve a desired result.

Harold Holt Rhyming slang for bolt, or flee. It refers to a former Australian Prime Minister who disappeared while swimming at a Victorian beach in 1967.

Harry High Pants A nickname for anyone whose pants are pulled too high above their waist.

hash cookies Biscuits made with hashish in them.

hassle A problem or inconvenience.

hat rack A thin or scrawny animal. Also used to refer to people who are thin.

hats off to ... Congratulations to.

hatter A lonely and eccentric bush resident. Was originally a miner who worked alone.

have 1. To fight someone, e.g. 'I'll have him one day'. 2. To have sex with someone.

have a bo-peep To take a look.

have a burl To attempt something.

have a cow To become upset.

have a gander To take a look.

have a go To make a determined effort.

have a good head for radio To have an unattractive head. Also **I've seen a better head on a glass of beer**.

have a good innings To have a long life or a long and successful career.

have a prang To have a car accident.

have a shot at 1. To attack verbally. 2. To make an attempt.

have by the short and curlies To have someone at your mercy. Also **have by the short hairs**.

have had Totally fed up with something, e.g. 'I've had enough of this joint'.

have hollow legs Having a prodigious appetite for food or alcohol.

have it off To have sex.

have the painters in To have your menstrual cycle.

have tickets on yourself Having an inflated view of yourself.

have to line him up with a strainer post to see if he's still moving Of someone who hasn't moved for a while or who is very slow at doing things.

have your shit together To be in control of a situation.

Hawkesbury Rivers Rhyming slang for shivers.

hawk the fork To work as a prostitute.

hay burner A horse.

Hay, Hell and Booligal Anywhere that is hot and uncomfortable. Taken from the Banjo Paterson poem with all three names referring to places on the south-west plains of NSW.

head case A nut case.

head down and arse up To be busy working.

head honcho The boss or a person in charge.

headless chicken To **run around like a headless chicken** is to act in a haphazard manner, without rhyme or reason. Also **headless chook**.

headlights The breasts. Also refers to erect nipples.

head like a ... An ugly head and used in the following phrases: **head like a half-sucked mango** and, worse, **head like a half-sucked mango and a body like a burst sausage**, **a head like a half-sucked Cheezel**, **head like a dropped meat pie**, **head like a racing tadpole**, **head like a revolving mallee root**, **head like a Turkish trotting duck**, **head like a chewed Mintie** and **head like a busted sofa**.

head over turkey To fall head over heels or arse over tit.

head rush A sudden sensation in the head as caused by a rush of adrenaline.

head serang or **sherang** The person in charge or the boss.

headshrinker A psychiatrist. Also shortened to **shrink**.

head swell A conceited person.

head-turner An attractive person

heap An old, dilapidated car.

heaps 1. A lot or many, e.g. 'There were heaps of people at the footy'. 2. An intensifier, e.g. 'She loves me heaps'. 3. To **give someone heaps** is to strongly reprimand them.

heap shit on To criticise harshly.

heart-starter An early morning alcoholic drink.

heave To vomit.

heave-ho Rejection, e.g. 'My boss has just given me the old heave-ho'.

heaven on a stick Something delicious and often used to refer to a sexually attractive person.

he can put his shoes under my bed any day Used by women to indicate they are sexually attracted to a man.

hector protector A protective covering used in cricket to protect the genitals.

heel A despicable or disliked person.

heeler A blue heeler dog.

heifer A derisive term for a woman.

heifer paddock A girl's school.

height challenged Short.

helicopter A dragonfly.

hellish An adolescent perversion of great or wonderful.

helluva An intensifier to denote a very good or extreme example, e.g. 'We had a helluva time at the party'.

helm or **at the helm** To be in charge of something.

he looks like he's been pulled through a hollow log backwards An unattractive man.

hen 1. A fussy woman. 2. A bride-to-be.

Henry the Third Rhyming slang for turd. Also **Richard the Third** and **William the Third**.

hen's night 1. A party for women and thrown for a bride-to-be before the wedding. 2. An evening when a group of women have a night out.

herbs Engine horsepower. Also fuel supplied for the engine.

he thinks he's God's gift to women A man who thinks he is charming and handsome, and whom women will flock around.

he went mad and they shot him Used as a reply when someone asks the whereabouts or wellbeing of someone else and you don't know the answer.

hey A greeting or a call to attract one's attention.

hey diddle diddle Rhyming slang for both middle and piddle.

hickey A mark caused by erotic sucking of the skin and usually on the neck. Also called a **love bite**.

hide Impudence. To have **more hide than Jessie** is to be extremely impudent. Jessie was an elephant at Sydney's Taronga Park Zoo.

hide-and-seek A children's game in which most hide and someone tries to find them. Also **hidies** or **hide-and-go-seek**.

high flyer Someone who is adept at taking marks in Aussie Rules.

high jump 1. To be **for the high jump** is to be up for trial, punishment or reprimand. 2. Execution by hanging.

highway robbery A rip off or extracting an exorbitant amount of money for something.

the **Hill** 1. A sloping area of ground for spectators at Flemington Racecourse. 2. The sloped area in front of the scoreboard at the Sydney Cricket Ground. 3. Shortened name for the city of Broken Hill in western NSW.

hip-pocket nerve An imaginary nerve that is sensitive when demands are made for your money.

hissy fit An hysterical attack or a tantrum.

hit and giggle Non-competitive or social tennis.

hit-and-run A game of cricket with the rule that each time the ball is hit by the bat, you have to run. Also known as **tip-and-run**, **tippety-run**, **tippy go**, **tippy-go-run**, **tipsy**, **tipsy-run**, **nick-and-run**, **snick-and-run** and **tip-and-go**.

hit for six To stun or confound.

hit the bottle To begin drinking.

hit the frog and toad To hit the road or to depart.

hit the hay or **hit the sack** To go to bed.

hit the nail on the head Getting something exactly right.

hit the piss To drink heavily.

hock To pawn or sell something.

hock a loogie To spit out a big golly.

hockey puck A disinfectant tablet placed in a urinal.

hoe into To undertake a task with vigour.

hog 1. A gluttonous or selfish person who takes more than a fair share. 2. A large motorcycle, usually a Harley-Davidson.

hoist To throw or chuck something.

holding A supply of ready cash.

hole 1. A dirty, cruddy or objectionable place. 2. Any aperture of the body, such as mouth, ear, nose or anus. 3. To **put a big hole in** something is to consume a large amount.

hols or **hollies** Abbreviation of holidays.

holy Moses An exclamation meaning 'Heavens above'. Also **holy boon-boon**, **holy snapping duckshit**, **holy Christ**, **holy Jesus**, **holy Mother**, **holy Mother of God**, **holy mackerel**, **holy moley**, **holy smoke**, **holy dooley** and **holy shit**.

home and hosed To be a long way in front in any form of race or sporting event.

home on the pig's back Certain to succeed.

homo Homosexual.

hon Short for honey, a term of endearment.

honcho The boss.

honey 1. A good-looking person, e.g. 'She's a real honey'. 2. A term of endearment. Also **honey bun**, **honey buns**, **honey bunch** and **honey pie**.

honey pot The vagina.

honker The nose.

hoodie A jacket with a hood.

hoof The foot.

hoof it To walk to a destination, e.g. 'The car won't start, we're going to have to hoof it'.

hoo-ha A fuss.

hook 1. To capture someone in marriage. 2. To illegally pull a horse in a race to prevent it from winning.

hooker A prostitute.

hooks Fingers.

hooley dooley An exclamation of surprise or amazement.

hoon 1. A reckless show-off or troublemaker. A hooligan or lout. 2. To drive recklessly.

hoop A jockey.

hooroo Goodbye. Often shortened to **ooroo**. Also **hooray**.

hoot Money.

hooter The nose.

hop head A drunk.

hop in for your chop To take your fair share.

hop into To tackle with gusto and enthusiasm.

Hopoate To goose the anus of another. After the goosing tactics of rugby league player John Hopoate.

hopper 1. A kangaroo or wallaby. 2. A grasshopper.

hops Beer.

horizontal folk dancing Sexual intercourse. Also **horizontal hula**.

horn 1. The telephone. 2. An erect penis. Something extremely arousing is said to be able to **put a horn on a jellyfish**.

hornbag Someone who is sexually attractive.

horny Sexually excited.

horse bite A slap to the bare skin with a cupped hand, usually on the legs, that really stings.

horse's doover A mispronunciation of hors d'oeuvre.

horse's hoof Rhyming slang for poof.

horsey A leap into the water with one leg tucked under your arms and hugged into the chest and the other extended out. It is intended to make a big splash. Also a **banana**, **can opener** or **peg leg**.

hospital pass In football, a pass to a player who is in imminent danger of being crash-tackled. In Aussie Rules a **hospital kick** is one that goes straight up in the air.

hostie Shortened version of air hostess. Nowadays they are called flight attendants.

hot 1. A sexually attractive member of the opposite sex. 2. Fashionable and exciting. 3. Performing well or at one's peak. 4. Stolen or illegally obtained property. 5. Wanted by the police. 6. The latest.

hot pot A favourite in a horse or dog race.

hots To have a strong sexual attraction to someone.

hot shit 1. An expert or someone who is proficient at something. 2. Enthusiasm or excitement.

hot shot A proficient person.

hot stuff 1. An attractive person. 2. Someone or something of great interest.

hottie 1. A hot-water bottle. 2. A good-looking woman.

hot to trot Ready to go.

hot-wire To start an engine using a wire to bypass the starting key.

the house that Jack built A sexual diseases clinic, with Jack being another name for venereal disease.

how's it goin? A form of greeting. Also **how ya goin?** or **how ya travelling?**

how's it hanging? How are you? Usually used among men and referring to the genitalia. Also **how are they hanging?** or **how's your left testicle?**

how would you be? A greeting.

howzat 1. An appeal for approval. 2. An appeal made in cricket to ask the umpire whether or not a batsman is out.

hoy 1. To throw. 2. A call, e.g. 'I'll give them a hoy now'. 3. A game of chance using playing cards.

hubby The husband.

Huey A name for the heavenly powers that supposedly control the weather. Particularly used in reference to rain, e.g. 'Send her down Huey'. Also spelt **Hughie**.

hum If something is a bit smelly it has a bit of a hum.

humbug 1. Nonsense. 2. To annoy. 3. To beg or cadge.

hump 1. To carry something. 2. Sexual intercourse.

hump the bluey To live the life of a swagman.

humpy A rough bush shelter.

humungous Something that is very big.

hung A male possessing a large penis. Used in sayings like **hung like a donkey** or **hung like an elephant**.

hungry bum Pants that have crept into the butt cleft.

hunky dory Satisfactory or splendid. Often shortened to hunky.

hurdy-gurdy A merry-go-round or carousel.

hurl To vomit.

hurry up A call to action, e.g. 'Why don't you give them a hurry up?'

husband beater A long, narrow loaf of bread.

hush money A bribe to keep quiet about something.

hydro 1. Short for hydroelectric. 2. Hydroponically grown marijuana.

hyper Overstimulated, overexcited or overactive.

the **Hypodermic** Refers to the Telstra Tower in Canberra.

I

ice 1. A crystallised form of methamphetamine. 2. Diamonds.

iceberg A person who swims regularly during winter.

ice-cold A cold beer, e.g. 'I think it's time for a few ice-colds'.

ice queen A woman who is very cold towards anyone.

identity An interesting person or a character.

idiot box The television.

idiot lights The warning lights on the dashboard of a vehicle.

iffy Something that is suspicious, risky or doubtful.

if he fell into a barrel of tits he'd come up sucking his thumb Someone of dubious intelligence.

if it moves shoot it, if it doesn't chop it down A summary of the Australian attitude to clearing and settling the land.

if it was raining palaces I'd be hit on the head with a dunny door A phrase indicating someone's misfortune or bad luck. Also **if it was raining virgins I'd be locked in the dunny with a poofter** or **if it was raining soup I'd have a fork**.

if you've got it flaunt it An appeal to use your best assets to your advantage.

I kid you not An expression emphasising that something is very true.

illywhacker A con artist or swindler.

imaginitis Having an overactive imagination.

I'm all right Jack A term generally used to indicate that everyone is out for whatever they can get with little or no regard for others.

imbo Short for imbecile.

improv Short for improvisation.

in 1. In children's games the person who must catch the others is described as the one who is 'in'. Also described as 'it'. 2. Assured of sexual success.

in a tic Very shortly.

inbreeder Derogatory term for a person from a remote area.

incoming A warning that something thrown is approaching.

indeedy Certainly. Also **indeedy-do**.

in fine feather Healthy, full of vitality and spirit.

in good nick In good condition.

ink Alcohol. To be **inked** is drunk.

in like Flynn A phrase indicating success in an endeavour or a sexual encounter and referring to Errol Flynn.

in more trouble than Speed Gordon is to be in trouble or dire straits. **In more shit than a Werribee duck** is primarily used in Victoria. It has a similar meaning and comes from the fact that Melbourne's sewerage treatment works are in Werribee.

innie A recessed belly button as opposed to an 'outie'.

innings 1. The period in which a team bats in cricket. 2. A period of time pertaining to humans, e.g. 'He had a really good innings'.

insane Among young people this is used to mean terrific or wonderful.

inside In prison.

intestinal fortitude Strength of will, determination and guts.

in the altogether In the nude.

in the buff Naked.

in the chair To be the person buying the drinks.

in the doghouse To be in disgrace or unpopular. Mostly used in relationships, to express your partner's displeasure with you (e.g. 'I'm in the doghouse with Jane'.)

in the know Having inside information about something.

in the nick Naked. Also **in the nuddy**.

in the pudding club Said of someone who is pregnant.

in the raw Naked.

in the shit To be in trouble. Also **in deep shit**.

in the sticks In remote areas in the bush, e.g. 'He lives out in the sticks'.

in the wars To be experiencing a time of trouble, illness or difficulty.

intro Abbreviation of introduction.

in two shakes A short time, e.g. 'I'll be there in two shakes'. Shortened from **in two shakes of a duck's** or **lamb's tail**.

invo Abbreviation of invitation.

in your dreams Not on your life or never, and indicating that whatever it is will only happen in the other person's dreams.

in-your-face Someone who is confronting.

Irish 1. Shortened version of Irish jig, which is rhyming slang for wig. 2. Illogical. 3. If you **get your Irish up** then you become angry.

Irish as paddy's pigs To be very Irish in character.

Irish curtains Cobwebs.

iron out 1. To straighten a problem or issue out. 2. Knocking someone out.

iron pony A motorcycle.

the **irrits** Irritated or annoyed.

the **Isa** The Queensland mining town of Mount Isa.

Is the Pope a Catholic? Rhetorical question to emphasise that something is correct.

it 1. Sex appeal. 2. Sexual intercourse. 3. The person chosen for a specific task, e.g. 'All right, you're it'. 4. In children's games the person who must catch everyone else.

Italian lawn The areas of concrete that often fill the yards of the homes of people with a Mediterranean background. Also **Lebanese lawn**.

item Describes a romantic relationship between two people, e.g. 'Gary and Michelle are an item'.

Itie Disparaging term for an Italian. Also spelt **Eyetie**.

it's not over till the fat lady sings The outcome is not known until the very end.

I've had it Frustration, e.g. 'I've had it with him'.

ivories 1. Teeth. 2. To **tickle the ivories** is to play the piano.

J

jack 1. Venereal disease. 2. A police officer or detective. 3. Nothing. A shortening of **jack shit**. 4. An increase, e.g. 'The waves jacked again this morning'.

Jack and Jill Rhyming slang for bill. Also can be used for pill, dill and till.

jackass 1. The kookaburra. 2. A person who does silly or stupid things.

Jack Dancer Rhyming slang for cancer and often shortened to dancer.

jacked up 1. To refuse to do something. 2. Infected with venereal disease.

jacked off Annoyed.

jackeroo A young male apprentice station hand.

jack-in-the-box Someone who cannot keep still.

jackjumper A Tasmanian name for an aggressive bull ant with a very nasty bite. Also called **hopper ants** or **jumper ants**.

Jack Lang Rhyming slang for Australian slang.

jacko The kookaburra.

jack of To be fed up with something.

jack off To masturbate.

jack shit Knowing nothing or getting nothing.

jack up 1. To refuse to do something. 2. To increase something.

Jacky A nickname given to Aboriginal men by white people. Shortened from **Jacky Jacky**.

Jacky Howe A navy or black woollen singlet named after a world champion shearer of 1892.

jaffa 1. A very good delivery in cricket. 2. An acronym with many uses, including Just Another Fucking Field Assistant, in mining; Just Another Fat Fucking Arsehole; Just Another Fucking Accountant. 3. A chocolate sweet covered with an orange coating.

jaffle A toasted sandwich cooked in a jaffle iron.

jaffy An annoying first-year student at a tertiary institution. An acronym for Just Another Fucking First-year.

jag 1. A drinking binge or any sustained activity. 2. To catch something. Also **jagged**.

jail bait A girl or boy below the legal age of consent.

jake 1. All right, e.g. 'She'll be jake'. 2. A toilet.

jam tart A good-looking young woman. It was originally rhyming slang for sweetheart.

Jap A shortening of Japanese.

Japanese riding boots or **Japanese safety boots** A pair of thongs. Also called **Chinese safety boots**. These are ironic terms as they are often made in Asia from cheap rubber and/or plastic and are unsuitable as footwear for safety or riding.

Jap crap Japanese cars and other goods made in Japan.

Japper Derogatory term for a Japanese motorcycle.

jar 1. A glass of beer. 2. To upset someone with an insult or cutting remark.

jarmies Pyjamas.

J Arthur Masturbation. Short for J Arthur Rank, rhyming slang for wank.

Jatz crackers The testicles. Rhyming slang for knackers.

jaw-breaker A hard-to-chew piece of candy or a long word that is difficult to pronounce.

Jeff's Shed A derisive name in Victoria for the Melbourne Exhibition Centre and named after former premier Jeff Kennett.

jerk An annoying person.

jerk the gherkin To masturbate.

jerry 1. A chamber pot. If you are as **full as a family jerry** then you are completely full. 2. An old person. A shortening of geriatric. 3. During both World Wars a German was called a Jerry. 4. If you **jerry to** something or **take a jerry to** it then you understand it.

Jerusalem screw A brutal and hard prison warder. This term originated in World War I when the British in Palestine trained Aussies in the art of breaking particularly tough prisoners.

Jesus bird The comb-crested jacana or lily walker, so called because it walks on water. Also **Christ bird.**

Jesus freak An enthusiastic Christian.

Jesus handle A fixed handle inside a vehicle that is grabbed by passengers when in fear, that is, when they might exclaim 'Jesus!'.

jet To leave or depart, e.g. 'I'll jet off now'.

jeweller's shop A rich deposit of gold or opal.

jewels The testicles. Also the **crown jewels** or the **family jewels**.

jezza An extremely spectacular mark in Aussie Rules and named after champion player Alex Jesaulenko.

jiffy A short time, e.g. 'I'll be back in a jiffy'.

jig To play truant.

jigger 1. What you call a device when you can't think of its name. 2. An illegal crystal radio set in prison. 3. An illegal device in horseracing that gives the horse a shock during a race. 4. An electric cattle prod.

jiggered 1. No longer useful. 2. Completely exhausted.

jillaroo A female station hand.

Jimmy Brits Rhyming slang for the shits and can mean diarrhoea or being in a bad mood.

Jimmy Riddle Rhyming slang for piddle, or urination.

Jimmy Woodser A person who drinks alone in a bar.

jingoes An exclamation of surprise. Often used as **by jingoes**.

jism Semen. Also spelt **gism**, **jissom** and **jizzom**. Shortened to **jizz**.

Joan of Arc Rhyming slang for shark.

job 1. To hit or punch somebody, e.g. 'Watch out or I'll job you'. 2. The product of defecation. Used by children and when directed to children it is as a **big job**.

jobs for the boys Preferential treatment for your friends.

jock A contemptible homosexual man.

jocks Male underpants.

Joe Blake Rhyming slang for snake.

Joe Blakes Rhyming slang for the shakes.

Joe Bloggs or **Joe Blow** The great Australian anybody or the average man in the street.

joes A fit of depression or irritation.

joey Baby kangaroo.

john 1. The toilet. 2. A police officer. An abbreviation of *gendarme*. 3. The client of a prostitute.

John Dory Rhyming slang for story.

John Hop Rhyming slang for cop.

Johnny Bliss Rhyming slang for piss.

Johnny Cash Rhyming slang for hash.

Johnny Raper Rhyming slang for newspaper.

jo-jo In WA the lawn weed known elsewhere as bindi-eye.

joke A person who is laughable and not to be taken seriously.

joker A fellow or a bloke, e.g. 'He's a weird sort of joker'.

jollies Cheap thrills, e.g. 'He gets his jollies watching wet T-shirt competitions'.

jonnic Genuine or true but now seldom used.

josh To joke in a teasing manner.

journo Shortening of journalist.

joystick The penis.

the Js National ABC radio station Triple J.

jug Slang term for a glass of beer.

jugs The breasts.

juice 1. Fuel used for an engine. 2. Power. 3. Any alcoholic beverage. 4. A sexual secretion.

juicy fruit Rhyming slang for root as an act of sexual intercourse.

jumbuck A sheep.

jump 1. To board public transport without paying the fare. 2. Sexual intercourse. 3. The bar in a pub. 4. The start of a race, e.g. 'At the jump he was first to lead'.

jumper An Aussie word for a sweater or jersey.

jump the twig To die.

jump-up A point where the country rises abruptly from one level to another or a sharp rise in flat country. Jump-up country is the area around Tibooburra in north-west NSW.

jumpy as a wallaby Someone who is very nervous.

jungle juice A rough, strong and generally inexpensive alcoholic drink.

junk Heroin.

junkie 1. A drug addict. 2. Addicted to anything, such as a chocolate junkie or an ice-cream junkie.

JW A member of the Jehovah's Witness faith.

K

k's Shortening of kilometres.

Kal Shortening of the WA town of Kalgoorlie.

kalamazoo In WA a hand-pumped railway trolley used by fettlers.

kamikaze 1. A reckless or dangerous act or a reckless person. 2. In surfing a deliberate wipe-out.

Kanaka A derogatory term for a Pacific Islander.

kanga 1. Shortening of kangaroo. 2. Money. 3. Prison rhyming slang for screw as in prison warder.

kangaroo 1. To make a car jump along through poor use of the clutch is to kangaroo hop. 2. To squat over a toilet without touching the seat.

kangaroos loose in the top paddock Used to describe someone considered crazy or mad.

Kangaroo Valley The London suburb of Earls Court where many Australians gather.

Kate's Folly Bruce Stadium in Canberra. Named after Kate Carnell, Chief Minister of the ACT from 1995–2000.

keen as mustard Very enthusiastic. Based on the Keen's brand of mustard.

keep nit To act as a lookout.

keg on legs A heavy drinker.

kelly An axe.

Kembla Grange Rhyming slang for change, as in money.

Kenmore tractor Brisbane slang for a four-wheel-drive only used in the city.

'kenoaf A euphemistic variation of 'fucking oath'.

Kentucky Labor pack A derogatory term for Labor Party supporters and members. It describes a certain brand of takeaway food that would be full of left wings and parson's noses for ALP buyers.

kerb crawling Driving a car slowly along seeking sexual partners.

kero Abbreviation of kerosene.

kewl A young person's variation on cool or extra cool. Also **kewlies**.

Khyber Pass Rhyming slang for the arse.

kick 1. A pocket in the trousers. To **hit the kick** is to reach into the pocket for money. 2. An Aussie Rules player viewed in terms of his kicking skills. 3. A sudden burst of speed.

kick arse or **kicks arse** To be totally amazing, e.g. 'The team really kicked arse today'. Also **kick butt**.

Kickastickalong or **Kickatinalong** An imaginery remote country town.

kick back To relax.

kick for the other team To be homosexual.

kick in To contribute to the cause.

kick in the teeth A setback.

kick off To start.

kick on To continue.

to **kick the arse off an emu** To feel in tip-top shape, ready to tackle anything.

kick the bucket To die.

kick the tin To make a donation.

kick up the arse A severe scolding. **Better than a kick up the arse** is a dry sign of appreciation.

kid's beer 1. Low alcohol beer. 2. The KB brand of beer.

kidstakes Kidding around or childish behaviour.

kiff Marijuana.

kill a brown dog Repulsive food is said to be able to kill a brown dog.

kill a snake To urinate.

killer 1. Fantastic, e.g. 'He played a killer game'. 2. An animal about to be slaughtered.

Killiecrankie diamond A colourless topaz found near a town of the same name on Flinders Island.

kill the pig To work very hard.

kinder or **kindy** Kindergarten.

king 1. Excellent. 2. An expert at something, e.g. 'He was a euchre king'. 3. To king someone is to king-hit them.

the **King** Champion Queensland and Australian rugby league player Wally Lewis.

king brown A 750ml bottle of beer. Also called a **longneck** or a **tallie**.

king dick or **king shit** A term used by others to describe someone who thinks they are better than everyone else.

king hit Originally a knockout blow but now a cowardly attack from behind. A king-hit merchant is a cowardly thug.

kingie 1. A king prawn. 2. A kingfish.

king of the ring A prominent bookmaker.

king pair The dismissal of a batsman in cricket on the first ball of both innings.

kingpin The top person in an organisation.

King River prawn Melbourne slang for a piece of human excrement floating in the ocean.

king's ransom A huge amount of money.

kip 1. A short nap. 2. The piece of wood used in the game of two-up.

kipper A sailor in the Royal Navy but used by Australians to describe any English person.

kiss arse To crawl or pander to someone in authority.

KISS method A simple method of explaining things. It stands for Keep It Simple Stupid.

kiss my arse A derisive expression, Also **kiss my bum, kiss my quoit** or **kiss my ring**.

kite 1. A spinnaker. 2. An aeroplane. 3. Prison slang for a newspaper. 4. Underworld slang for a blank cheque.

kittle The collection of empty bottles that accumulates on a table during a drinking session.

Kiwi A New Zealander.

Kiwiland New Zealand.

klicks or **clicks** Kilometres.

klutz A clumsy or awkward person.

knackered 1. Tired or exhausted. 2. Suffering an injury to the testicles.

knackers The testicles.

knee trembler Sexual intercourse while both partners are standing up.

knickers Underpants or panties.

knickers in a knot To become upset and generally used as 'Don't get your knickers in a knot'.

knob 1. The head of the penis. 2. A stupid or annoying person, as in a dickhead.

knobbies Speedos.

knob end The head of the penis and also used to describe a dickhead or a prick.

knob jockey Derisive name for a homosexual.

knock 1. To criticise or find fault with. 2. To exhaust. 3. To have sexual intercourse. 4. An innings in cricket.

knock about To roam about or lead an irregular existence.

knock around with To spend some time with someone.

knock back 1. A refusal. 2. To drink quickly, e.g. 'I knocked back a few beers'.

knock down To spend all of your wages from a seasonal job and generally by going on a drinking binge.

knockdown A formal introduction.

knocked up 1. Pregnant. 2. Tired or exhausted.

knock 'em down rains Violent thunderstorms in the north of Australia.

knocker 1. Someone who criticises or puts other people down. 2. To be **on the knocker** is to be precise.

knockers 1. The breasts. 2. A brothel.

knock for six To astound with an effort.

knocking shop or **knock shop** A brothel.

knock it off 1. Stop it. 2. To have sexual intercourse.

knock it on the head To put a stop to something.

knock off 1. Time to stop work. 2. To stop doing anything. 3. To steal. 4. To kill. 5. To complete something with ease and speed. 6. To have sexual intercourse. 7. To copy or fake something.

knock-off time The end of the working day.

knock out 1. To earn. 2. To produce something.

knock over 1. To drink. 2. To rob.

knockover An easy success.

knock rotten To stun with a heavy blow.

knock together To put something together hastily.

knock up 1. To exhaust or wear out. 2. To arouse by knocking. 3. In prison, to attract the attention of other by banging on the cell door. 4. To amass a good score in sport. 5. To make pregnant. 6. To put together something with haste.

know-all A person who likes displaying their knowledge to others. Also a **know-it-all**.

know your shit To know your subject well.

knuckle To hit someone with your fists. To **go the knuckle** is to fight and **to be fond of the knuckle** is to have a tendency to solve your difference using your fists.

knucklehead A fool.

knuckles A game in which the two contestants hold closed fists knuckle to knuckle and take turns at hitting the other's knuckles.

knuckle sandwich A punch.

kook 1. A strange person. 2. A novice surfer.

kooka The kookaburra.

Kossy or **Kozzie** A shortened name for Australia's highest mountain Mt Kosciuszko.

Kraut A racist term for a German.

kybo A temporary toilet built for use when camping. It supposedly stands for Keep Your Bowels Open.

kybosh To **put the kybosh on something** is to put an end to it or to upset someone's plans.

kylie A boomerang with one flat and one convex side.

L

lace-out A perfect kick in Aussie rules that delivers the ball to the marker with the lace facing outwards.

lacky band An elastic band. Also a lacky or a lacker band.

lad Originally just for a boy but now used for an adult man who behaves like a child and in a chauvinistic way. A group of male friends when out together is **the lads**.

la-de-da If you are perceived to be snobbish or pretentious you are said to be a bit la-de-da.

Lady Blamey In World War II a drinking glass made from an empty bottle with the top cut off.

lady in the boat A Coolibah wine cask, so called due to the picture on the side.

lady killer An attractive male.

Lady Muck or **Lord Muck** Pretentious or snobbish.

lady's waist A small, waisted glass used for serving alcoholic drinks.

lag 1. To transport a convict from Britain. Upon being freed a convict was then known as an old lag. 2. To report someone to the authorities. Also **lag on**.

lagerphone An Aussie musical instrument made by nailing bottle caps to a wooden stick which is then pounded on the floor or ground.

lagger A police informer.

laid back Relaxed or informal.

lair Someone who brags a lot and generally dresses in loud clothes to attract attention to himself. Also a **mug lair**.

lairise To act like a lair. Also **lair about**.

lairy Flashy.

la-la The toilet.

lambing down The practice of extracting the pay packet of seasonal workers by getting them drunk and keeping them that way until their money runs out.

lamington An Australian treat of sponge cake pieces dipped in chocolate and covered with coconut. Also **lammie** or **lammo**.

land To win in horseracing.

Landie A Landrover. Also a **Lannie**.

land lice Sheep.

Land of the Long Weekend Said of Australia because its residents can't wait for one to come along.

Land of the Long White Cloud New Zealand.

Land of the Wrong White Crowd The Sydney suburb of Bondi, which is home to many Kiwis and Poms.

langers Drunk.

La Perouse Rhyming slang for booze and named after the Sydney suburb of the same name.

lappies Circuits of a city or town block in a car for the purpose of entertainment or to impress onlookers. Also **blockies** or **bog laps.**

larrikin A good-natured and wild-spirited person usually with little regard for authority, or a young mischievous male.

Larry Dooley To give someone one of these is to give them a hiding or beating.

lash 1. To have a go at something, e.g. 'I'll have a lash at that'. 2. An act of sexual intercourse.

lash out To go on a spending spree.

later A shortening of 'I'll see you later'.

laughing To be in a favourable or fortunate position.

laughing gear The mouth. To wrap your laughing gear around something is to eat it.

laughing jackass The kookaburra.

laughing sides Elastic-sided boots.

laugh like a drain To laugh in a loud and undignified manner.

Laura Norda Strine for law and order.

lav or **lavvy** An outdoor toilet but now used to mean any toilet.

lay 1. To bet or wager. To **lay off** is to have a second bet on another competitor to offset money already wagered. 2. To have sex with someone. 3. To **crack a lay** is to divulge information.

lay a cable To defecate.

lay an egg To defecate.

lay down misere Something that is certain to happen.

lay in the hay To have sexual intercourse.

lazy wind A bitterly cold wind that is too lazy to go around you, going right through you instead.

lead swinger A lazy person.

Leagues Shortening for a licensed rugby league club.

leaguey A follower or player of rugby league.

leak To urinate.

leather dyke A homosexual woman who dresses in leather.

Leb A Lebanese person.

Lebanese lawn Concrete that commonly fills the front or back yards of the homes of Lebanese people. Also **Italian lawn**.

Leb chariot An old car that has been done up and usually with a loud stereo system.

ledge Short for legend, a cool person.

leery Suspicious or doubtful. A man scared of getting married is said to be **leery of the brush**.

left footer Anyone of Roman Catholic persuasion as seen by a Protestant and considered to be different from the norm, which is right footed.

leftie 1. Anyone with socialist ideals. 2. A left-handed or left-footed person. 3. A left turn in a vehicle. 4. A punch with the left fist.

left in the lurch To be abandoned in a time of need.

legend A cool person or someone you admire. Also **ledge**.

legend in your own mind Someone who is fabulously conceited but has no right to be.

leggie A leg spin delivery or a leg spin bowler in cricket.

leg it To decamp from the scene. Also simply to walk.

legit Short for legitimate. Genuine or truthful.

legless Very drunk.

leg man A male who is aroused by women's legs.

leg of lamb A cool person. An elaboration of the word legend.

Lego Land Any new suburb full of similar houses crammed together in streets and cul-de-sacs.

leg opener Alcohol, especially gin, that is meant to help in the seduction of women.

leg-over An act of sexual intercourse. To **get your leg over** is to have sex.

legs 1. The ability to keep going in sport. To **have legs** is to endure or go the distance. 2. Used by males to refer to women with nice legs. Also **she's got legs** and **she's got legs right up to her bum**.

Leichhardt grass Sydney slang for the concrete that commonly fills the front or back yards of people of Mediterranean background. There are many people of this background who live in the suburb of Leichhardt.

lemon 1. Something that is faulty. 2. A car that looks okay but is mechanically unsound. 3. A lesbian.

lemon head A surfie with bleached hair.

lemony Annoyed.

length A way of referring to the penis.

lesbie A lesbian. Also **lezzo**, **lezzie**, **lezzer** or **lesbo**.

lesbie friends A lesbian couple. Often used by schoolgirls to malign other girls who are close friends.

letch Disparaging term for a lecherous man or a womaniser.

let alone Not to mention.

let go To pass wind from the anus. Also **let one go** or **let off**.

let her rip A command to start something.

let rip 1. To allow to get angry or passionate. 2. To fart.

let's blow this popsicle stand To leave. Also **let's blow this candy store**.

leviathan A wealthy man who bets big.

lid A term for a hat.

lifer Someone sentenced to life imprisonment.

life sucks and then you die A phrase expressing a dismal outlook on life and generally used after having some misfortune. Also **life's a bitch and then you die**.

the **lights are on but nobody's home** Used to refer to someone without brains or who doesn't think.

like 1. As it were. Often put at the end of a phrase. 2. Used before a number to indicate proximity. 3. Used to emphasise a statement, e.g. 'He was a big bloke, like really big'. 4. Used by young people to introduce reported speech.

like a chook with its head cut off Flustered or erratic. Also **like a blue-arsed fly in a bottle**.

like a cocky looking down a biscuit tin Excited or eager.

like a cut snake Very agitated.

like a fart in a bottle Agitated.

like a hole in the head To not want something at all.

like a one-armed taxi driver with crabs Very busy.

like a pick pocket at a nudist camp Confused.

like a pigeon on to a piece of fat To move quickly to claim something.

like a pimple on a pumpkin Something that is very obvious.

like a rat up a drainpipe To do something with great speed.

like a shag on a rock To be alone.

like a stunned mullet Bewildered.

like a ton of bricks With great force.

like a two-bob watch Unreliable or making a fuss.

like an old maid's pram Empty.

like buggery No way.

lily on a dustbin Someone or something that is rejected or neglected.

limp dick A weak-willed or ineffectual male.

limp wristed A homosexual male.

line A pick-up line. To **do a line with someone** is to court them or date them.

lingo Language.

lip Cheek or backchat.

lippie Lipstick.

lipstick lesbian A lesbian who wears conventional women's clothing and make-up. Also **a lipstick dyke**.

liquid amber Beer.

liquid laugh Vomit.

liquid lunch To drink alcohol and not eat at lunchtime.

little Aussie battler A member of the working class in Australia.

little blister Rhyming slang for sister.

little boy A cocktail frankfurt. Also a **cheerio**.

little green cart The supposed vehicle that comes to take you away to a psychiatric institution.

little house The toilet. Also the **little boy's room** or **the little girl's room**.

Little House on the Prairie A nickname for Parliament House in Canberra.

little jobs Urination. Used when speaking to children.

Little Johnny A nickname for former Prime Minister John Howard, Also **Little Johnny Jackboots**.

little tacker A small child.

littlie A child.

live on the smell of an oily rag To survive on a bare amount of money and food. A car which runs on the smell of an oily rag is a very economical one.

Liverpool kiss A headbutt. Also **Balmain kiss**.

livestock Maggots infesting a dead body.

living shit A substitute for hell, e.g. 'He beat the living shit out of me'.

lizard The penis. Used in phrases such as **drain the lizard** to urinate, and **flog** or **gallop the lizard** to masturbate.

lizard drinking To be **flat out like a lizard drinking** is to be very busy.

load 1. A venereal infection. 2. An ejaculation of semen. 3. To get a load of something is to look at it, e.g. 'Get a load of that bird'.

loaded 1. Very wealthy. 2. Drunk. 3. Unjustly incriminated. 4. Stoned on drugs.

load up To falsely charge someone with crimes they didn't commit.

loaf Your head. Loaf of bread is rhyming slang for head.

lob 1. To arrive, especially unexpected, e.g. 'She lobbed in late for the party'. 2. To land. 3. To win a race.

lobster A $20 note, because of its colour.

the **local** Your local pub or drinking hole.

local rag The local newspaper.

local yokels Local inhabitants of a suburb or town.

logodile A half-submerged log mistaken for a crocodile.

lollipop 1. Rhyming slang for cop. 2. An easy delivery to hit in cricket.

lolly 1. To **do your lolly** is to lose your temper. 2. A sweet or candy. 3. Money.

lolly bags Speedos.

lolly legs Long skinny legs or a tall person with long legs.

lolly water 1. Carbonated soft drink. 2. A disparaging term for the alcoholic sweet spirit mixers that are so popular.

London to a brick Extremely likely, e.g. 'It's London to a brick that they'll be late'. This derives from the racing industry with a punter so certain of winning that he/she is willing to bet London to win a meagre brick, i.e. ten quid.

long as a wet weekend Something that takes a depressingly long period of time.

long drop 1. A type of pit toilet. 2. Slang for death by hanging.

long flat dog A crocodile.

long grass The edge of the town of Darwin, where large numbers of displaced Aboriginals live who are known as **long grassers** or **long grass people**.

long hair 1. A hippie. 2. An intellectual.

long in the tooth Old or elderly, e.g. 'He's too long in the tooth to be playing sport'.

longneck A 750ml bottle of beer. Also a **longie**, **tallie** or **king brown**.

the **long paddock** The roadsides of country highways and roads used for grazing stock.

long pockets, short arms Someone who is miserly with their money.

long streak of misery A tall and thin person who is often miserable.

long streak of pelican shit A disparaging way of referring to a tall, thin person.

long time no see A way of greeting someone you haven't seen in a long time.

Lonnie Shortened way of saying the Tasmanian town of Launceston.

loo The toilet.

The 'Loo The Sydney suburb of Woolloomooloo.

look a million dollars To look terrific.

looker An attractive person.

look like death warmed up To look poorly, especially someone who is ill.

look-see To examine something visually, e.g. 'I think I'll go have a look-see'.

looks like a drowned rat A skinny person who is very wet.

loony bin A psychiatric institution.

loop A crazy person or a weirdo.

loop-the-loop Rhyming slang for soup.

loopy Someone who is considered mad or even eccentric.

loppy A handyman on a station, also known as a **rouseabout**.

loser Someone who is hopeless at everything they attempt.

lose the plot To not understand what is going on.

lose your rag To lose your cool or get very angry.

love glove A condom.

love handles The roll of fat around the abdomen that can be easily grasped while having sex.

love juice Sexual secretions.

lovely An attractive woman.

love machine A passionate lover.

love muscle The penis.

lousy Not good, e.g. 'I'm feeling pretty lousy today'.

lower than a snake's belly A despicable, contemptible character. Also **lower than shark shit**.

low heel A derogatory term for a promiscuous woman or a prostitute. Shortened to **lowie**.

low-life 1. Society's seamy elements, such as those involved in vice. 2. A despicable person as used in 'you low-life scum'.

lowy A disparaging reference by young men of young women.

lubra An Aboriginal woman.

lubra lips Large lips.

lubricate the larynx To have a drink of alcohol.

luck out To have bad luck.

Lucky Country Australia is often described as the Lucky Country as it is seen as a fortunate nation enjoying the benefits of prosperity and opportunity.

lucky shop In Victoria, a TAB outlet.

lug 1. The ear. To chew someone's lug is to talk to them non-stop. 2. A big and clumsy person.

lumber To leave someone with something that is unwelcome, e.g. 'I'll have to lumber you with the groceries'.

lunatic soup Alcoholic drinks.

lunch 1. The male genitalia. Also **a packed lunch**. 2. If you **cut someone's lunch** you are making a move on their wife or girlfriend. This person is called a **lunch cutter**. 3. To **drop your lunch** or **open your lunch** is to pass wind.

lungs A crass term for breasts.

lurgy A cold or the flu. Common in the phrase **the dreaded lurgy**.

lurk An illegal or underhand racket.

lurk merchant Someone adept at organising lurks for personal gain.

lush 1. Sexually attractive. 2. As used by teenagers to mean terrific or wonderful. 3. A drunkard.

luv Often used as a substitute when you don't know a woman's name.

M

maaate A typically Australian, long drawn-out way of saying mate.

Mac attack The desire to eat at a McDonald's Family Restaurant.

macca A macadamia nut.

Maccas Abbreviation of McDonald's Family Restaurant or the food from such an establishment.

mad Exciting, very good or 'out there' and especially used by young people, e.g. 'Listen to this mad CD'.

mad as a cut snake To be mad in an angry sense or a crazy sense, or to behave wildly and erratically.

mad as a gum tree full of galahs To be all over the place.

mad as a meataxe To be crazy or act insanely.

mad mick Rhyming slang for a pick.

Madonna's bra A Sydney nickname for the Anzac Bridge which is said to resemble the pointy bra once worn by pop star Madonna.

mag To indulge in idle conversation.

maggered Very drunk.

maggies Magpies.

maggot 1. A loathsome person. 2. Drunk. Also **maggoted**.

maggot bag A meat pie. Also **maggot sack**.

maggots in white Aussie Rules umpires.

maggot taxi A sheep.

maggoty To be in a bad mood.

magic mushie Any of the mushrooms that contain an hallucinogenic substance.

magic sponge A sponge applied by trainers to supposedly injured sport players who then recover miraculously.

magnet 1. A person who attracts much interest from others due to their good looks and personality. 2. Any person or thing with the power to attract.

magsman 1. A good teller of stories. 2. A con man.

mail Inside information, e.g. 'He gave me some good mail on number two'.

Mainland In Tasmania, this refers to the other states of continental Australia.

main man Your best mate or someone for whom you have great admiration.

major 1. A goal in Aussie Rules worth six points as opposed to a behind, or minor, worth one. 2. As used by young people it means complete or total.

majorly In a major way or to a great extent.

make To seduce someone or to have sex.

make a blue To make a mistake.

make a botch of To mess up or botch something up.

make a proper galah of To make a fool of oneself.

make a quid To earn a living.

make babies To have sex but not necessarily for the purpose of producing children.

make do To cope, e.g. 'Don't worry about helping, I can make do'.

make feathers fly To cause a commotion.

make it To have sex.

make it snappy Hurry up.

make old bones To grow old.

make sheep eyes at To give adoring looks.

make tracks Leaving or departing, e.g. 'I'm gonna make tracks now'.

make waves To cause trouble.

make your marble good To improve your prospects.

makings 1. What it takes. 2. The tobacco and paper used to roll your own cigarette.

Malabar Hilton The Long Bay Correctional Complex in Malabar, Sydney.

malarky Foolish talk.

mallee A slang term for the outback. This refers to the mallee eucalypts that grow in dry bushland areas.

mallee bull To be **as fit as a mallee bull** is to be very fit and strong.

mallie Youths who continually hang around shopping centres and malls.

malt sandwich A beer.

man A general term of address to a man or a woman, e.g. 'Hey man, it's been a long time between drinks'. Young people often use phrases such as **my man**, to **be the man** and **my main man** in this manner.

man boobs The flabby contours of an overweight man's chest which look like boobs. Also **man boobies**, **man tits** or **bitch tits**.

mango madness A feeling of oppression suffered by residents of northern Australia in the lead-up to the wet season.

mangulate To mangle, wreck or twist out of shape.

man in white An Aussie Rules umpire.

manky Rotting, mouldy or repulsive.

man on the land A farmer, stockman or other rural worker who makes a living from the land.

a **man's not a camel** The desire to have an alcoholic drink before one 'dies of thirst'.

man-whore A man who sleeps around.

Maoriland New Zealand.

map of Tassie or **map of Tasmania** A woman's pubic area.

Maralinga breadbox A microwave oven.

margarine legs The legs of a promiscuous woman that are said to 'spread well'.

marijuana A slow-moving dope. Also an **opium**.

mark A person who is the target of a swindle. An **easy mark** is someone who easily falls prey to a joke, a con or a swindle.

marley A sideways skid on a bike.

Mary Pickford in three acts A quick wash of the face, hands and crotch.

masher A man who makes aggressive sexual advances to women.

Ma state New South Wales.

mate 1. The great Australian expression for a male friend or cobber. The bond is known as **mateship**. 2. Used to greet someone whose name you can't remember. 3. Increasingly used by women in referring to female friends.

mate's rates A discount given to a friend.

matey A variation of mate.

matilda A swag.

matinee Sexual intercourse in the afternoon. Also **afternoon delight**.

max Shortened version of maximum. **To the max** is to the utmost degree.

maxed out Surf that is too big to ride.

max out To reach the maximum.

mazuma Money.

me A traditional Aussie way of saying my, e.g. 'I'll just get me stubby holder'.

meat 1. Male or female genitalia. 2. People when considered as sexual objects, e.g. 'There'll be plenty of meat at the party'.

meat hangers A term for Speedos, or men's swimming briefs, commonly used in Queensland.

meat head An idiot or a fool.

meat market A venue where casual sex partners are easily found.

meat pie 1. The traditional national dish of Australia. Also **as Aussie as meat pies**. 2. Rhyming slang for eye.

meat-pie bookmaker A small-time bookmaker.

meat tag An identity disc worn by people in the armed forces. Also **a meat ticket**.

meat wagon An ambulance.

meet An appointment.

megababe A very attractive person who can be female or male.

megahunk A very attractive man.

mellow To relax or chill out.

melon 1. The head. 2. A fool or stupid person. Also **melonhead**.

melons Large breasts.

member The penis.

men in white The fictional employees of a psychiatric institution and those who take people away to the institution. It is used as a threat when someone is acting crazy.

mental 1. Driven to distraction or acting in a crazy manner. To **chuck a mental** is to lose your temper. 2. Very drunk. 3. Among young people it is used to describe a stupid person.

merchant A person noted for an aspect of their behaviour, e.g. a panic merchant.

mermaid A weighbridge inspector. So named because they are scaly.

meself The traditional Aussie way of saying 'myself'.

messages Small errands to the shop or other locations.

metalhead A heavy metal music fan.

Met cop A ticket inspector on the public transport system in Melbourne.

metho Methylated spirits.

Metho A person of the Methodist faith.

Methodist gate A gate that is very difficult to open — only a Methodist could open it without swearing.

Mexican Anyone from south of the state border.

Mick Anyone of Irish descent or of Roman Catholic persuasion.

mickey drip A Roman Catholic.

Mickey Finn A drink spiked with an incapacitating drug.

Mickey Mouse 1. Wonderful or excellent. Rhyming slang for grouse. 2. A mechanical item that is cheap and poorly made.

micky 1. The female genitalia. 2. A young, wild bull. 3. A tantrum and usually seen in the form to **chuck a micky**. 4. To **take the micky out of someone** is to tease them.

middy A 285ml beer glass in NSW, the ACT, WA, NT and parts of Queensland. It is called a **pot** in Victoria, Tasmania and Queensland, a **ten** in parts of Tasmania and Queensland, and, confusingly, a **schooner** in SA.

miffed To be upset or angry.

Mildura marching girls The tough roots of the bush mallee tree.

milk bar A corner shop selling milk, bread, sweets and groceries.

milko A person who delivers milk. Also **milkie**.

Ming the Merciless A nickname for long-serving Prime Minister Sir Robert Menzies.

min min light A mysterious type of bright light seen at night in the outback.

minnow A small-time gambler or a small-time player.

mint 1. Terrific or cool. Mainly used in WA. Also **mintox**. 2. Money.

as **miserable as a bandicoot on a burnt ridge** Very unhappy.

misery guts A person who is always complaining.

missus One's wife or partner.

mitt The hand.

mix and match Swear words.

mix it To fight.

mix up A fight or dispute.

mizzle off To leave.

mo 1. A short period of time, e.g. 'I'll be back in a mo'. Also **half a mo**. 2. A moustache.

mob 1. A crowd of people. 2. A group of people, perhaps friends, but not necessarily large. 3. If there are **mobs of** something there are large numbers of it. Also a **big mob**.

mobile Ready to leave at once.

mocca A Melbourne slang term for a westie, bogan or bevan.

moccas Shortening of moccasins.

mocker If you **put the mocker on** something you are hoping bad luck will befall it. Also **put the mockers on** or **put the mocks on**.

mods Modifications to a standard car engine.

mofo A euphemistic way of saying mother fucker.

moggy A cat.

moi French for me but often used in Australia in mock affectation.

moisty A nubile young girl.

moke A horse.

moll A promiscuous woman or a prostitute. Also **mole**. Something obviously in the wrong place is **like a moll at a christening**.

moll patrol A derogatory term for a group of schoolgirls as viewed by a rival group.

molly dooker A left hander.

mollycoddle To pamper or make a fuss over.

Molly the Monk Rhyming slang for drunk.

molo Drunk.

Mondayitis The dreadful lethargic feeling experienced on Monday morning upon returning to work after a great weekend.

money for jam Money that is easily made or won.

mong 1. A stupid person or a dork. This is a shortening of mongoloid. Also **monger**, **mongo** and **mongy**. 2. A mongrel dog.

monger Food or tucker.

mongrel 1. A despicable or despised person or thing, e.g. 'The mongrel car won't start'. 2. Something difficult.

mongulated Very stupid.

moniker 1. A person's name. 2. A person's signature.

monkey suit A dinner suit.

monobrow One long eyebrow across both eyes and the top of the nose.

monster To harass.

month of Sundays A long time, e.g. 'That job won't be done for a month of Sundays'.

monty A certainty.

moo A stupid person.

mooch 1. To loiter about. 2. To slouch or to saunter along.

moo juice Milk.

moolah Money.

moon or **mooning** The act of dropping your trousers and exposing your buttocks in public.

moonbeam A plate, cup or piece of cutlery not used at an evening meal and which does not need washing up.

moonface A person with a large round head.

moonie A public display of the buttocks.

moon tan The very pale skin of a person whose flesh barely sees sunlight.

moon unit An airhead or someone lacking intelligence.

moo poo Cow manure.

moosh 1. The mouth. 2. Prison food.

moot The female genitalia.

mop The hair, e.g. 'She's got a great mop of hair'.

moral Something that is certain, e.g. 'It's a moral to win'.

more front than Myers Someone who is very impudent. This comes from the Melbourne department store that has a large street frontage.

morning glory 1. Sexual intercourse upon awakening in the morning. 2. An erection of the penis upon awakening. 3. A horse that only performs well in morning trackwork.

Moscow A pawn shop. **To Moscow** something is to pawn it. There are many pawn shops in Moscow.

mosey To amble or stroll.

mosh To dance vigorously in a packed crowd in front of a stage. The area where this takes place is called a **mosh pit**. A **mosher** is someone who takes part in **moshing**, also a **moshie**.

Mosman tractor Sydney slang for a four-wheel-drive only used in the city.

motherless Completely hopeless or destitute and usually used as **stone motherless last** or **stone motherless broke**.

mother's milk Any form of beer or alcohol that is most favoured by the drinker.

motorhead A car enthusiast.

motormouth Someone who won't stop talking.

motza or **motser** A large amount of money, usually won in gambling.

mountain maggot A sheep.

mountain oyster The testicle of a bull or ram that is eaten as food. Also **prairie oyster**.

Mount Isa by the Sea A nickname for the Queensland city of Townsville and coined owing to its lack of greenery.

mouse potato Someone addicted to surfing the Internet.

mouth like the bottom of a cocky's cage A mouth that feels as if it is full of grit, which usually occurs after a big night of drinking.

move A choice or decision, e.g. 'That's a good move'.

move it, or lose it A warning made that whatever is in the road should by moved.

mow someone's lawn To have sex with another's partner. Also to **cut someone's grass**.

mozz Hoping that someone will make a mistake or come into bad luck.

mozzie or **mossie** The mosquito.

Mrs Kerfoops A fictitious woman used as a response to a question you can't answer or don't want to answer. She is also used as a scapegoat, e.g. 'Who used the last of the coffee?' 'Mrs Kerfoops did.' It is also used as a term of endearment to a young lady and sometimes as **Madame Kerfoops or Lady Kerfoops**. Can also be spelt **Kuffoops** or **Kafoops**.

Mrs Palmer and her five lovely daughters A metaphor for the hand that is used in male masturbation.

muchly Very much.

mucking around or **about** Fooling around or playing the goat.

muck up To make a mistake at something.

muddie A mudcrab.

mud gecko A crocodile.

mudguard A nickname for a stupid or silly bald man — shiny on top and shit underneath.

mud lark or **mud runner** 1. A horse that goes well in wet and heavy racetrack conditions. 2. Another name for the magpie lark or peewee.

mud map A map drawn in the earth with a stick. This is commonly used in the bush.

mud stump A termite mound.

muff 1. Female private parts. A **muff-diver** or a **muff-muncher** is someone who engages in cunnilingus. 2. A failure. 3. To make an error or mistake when doing something.

mug 1. The face. 2. A fool. 3. A criminal's victim. 4. A prostitute's client.

mug lair A flashy young man who uses brash or vulgar behaviour.

mugs away Indicates that the losers will go first in a game or contest.

mug's game A foolish or silly occupation or pastime, in other words something that a mug is likely to become involved in.

mulga A general term for the outback.

mulga wire The bush telegraph.

mullet 1. A hairstyle with the sides cut short and the back left long. 2. A stupid person.

mullock Rubbish or nonsense. To **poke mullock at** is to ridicule.

mullygrubber In cricket this is a low delivery that barely gets above the ground and usually bounces more than once before it reaches the batsman.

mumble pants Very tight-fitting gym shorts worn by women.

mummy's boy A male who is mollycoddled by his mother.

munchie A shark.

munchies 1. Anything to eat but particularly referring to snacks between meals. 2. A craving for food.

munchkin Someone who is small in stature.

mundowie The foot or a footprint. Used mainly in north Queensland.

mung 1. Food. 2. A fool or stupid person. 3. Under the influence of marijuana.

munga Food.

mung bean 1. A stupid person or a loser. 2. A greenie, vego or feral type.

mungo Derogatory term for a rugby league player.

mung out To eat.

munted 1. Ruined or wrecked. 2. The state you are in if you have too much alcohol or drugs.

Murray magpie An SA term for a magpie lark or peewee.

Murrumbidgee whaler A swaggie who toured around the inland rivers and sustained himself by begging and fishing.

muscle car A souped-up or hotted-up car.

muscle Mary A strong and masculine homosexual male.

muscles on your piles This is said of a very strong man.

mushie A mushroom.

mushroom Someone who is deliberately kept misinformed or in the dark, in other words 'they are kept in the dark and fed shit'.

mute Very drunk.

mutt 1. A dog. 2. A stupid or simple person.

mutton The penis.

my arse No way, I think not.

my bloody oath Certainly. Also **my oath**.

my dogs are barking Exclaimed by someone with sore feet.

mystery bag 1. A sausage. 2. A meat pie. Also a **mystery box**.

my word Certainly.

myxo Abbreviation of the rabbit control disease myxomatosis. Also called **myxie**.

N

nads The testicles. Shortened from gonads.

nag 1. A horse. 2. To spend **a day at the nags** is to go to the horse races.

name-dropper Anyone who always uses the names of famous people they have met, or supposedly met, in order to make themselves look good.

nana 1. Short for banana. 2. To **do your nana** is to lose your temper or throw a tantrum. Also **chuck a nana** or **doing your nana**. To be **off your nana** is to be crazy.

nancy boy An effeminate male. Also a **nancy**.

nanny goat Rhyming slang for the tote, as in totalisator.

Nappy Valley A derisive name for Tuggeranong in the ACT owing to the high birth rate there.

narc A police officer from the narcotics squad.

nard A piece of excrement.

nark 1. A police informer. 2. A person who is always whingeing. 3. To irritate or annoy.

narky Irritable or short tempered.

Nasho Abbreviation for a National Serviceman.

natch Abbreviation of naturally.

naughty An act of sexual intercourse.

Nazi Anyone with a dictatorial attitude about a certain topic or thing.

NBG No bloody good.

near and far Rhyming slang for bar.

neck To commit suicide by hanging.

neck-oil Alcohol, because it lubricates the throat.

neddy A horse. The **neddies** are the horse races.

Ned Kelly 1. The name of Australia's most famous bushranger is also used to refer to anyone who is a bit of a crook or a person who stands up courageously against authority. To be as **game as Ned Kelly** is to be gutsy. If you are **in more shit than Ned Kelly** then you are in big trouble. 2. Rhyming slang for belly.

need your head read means you are acting insanely or making an outlandish statement.

neenish tart A small tart with a pastry base, a dob of jam at the bottom, mock cream filling and a topping of icing with half in one colour and half in another, often white or pink and chocolate.

neg driving Shortened form of negligent driving.

nellie Cheap red wine.

Nellie Bly or **Nelly Bligh** Rhyming slang for meat pie or the fly of a pair of pants, or a lie or a tie.

nerd A geek, drongo or dag.

nervous Nelly Someone who is overly timid or nervous.

nest The vagina. To be **on the nest** is to be having sex.

net head An Internet addict.

netiquette Internet etiquette.

netizen A frequent user of the Internet.

never-never 1. The most remote areas of the outback. 2. The hire purchase system of buying goods.

Neville An unpopular person or a dag. Also **Nigel**.

newbie A newcomer.

new chum 1. A newcomer or an inexperienced person, e.g. 'He's a new chum on the job.' 2. Any new arrival to Australia from Britain.

newie Something that is completely new or a novelty.

NFI No fucking idea.

Niagaras Abbreviation of **Niagara Falls** which is rhyming slang for balls.

nibble pie A party pie.

nibs A title for an important person or a self-important person and often used in an ironical manner.

nice try, but no cigar A good but incorrect guess, answer or effort. Also **nice try, but no banana**. If the guess or answer is correct the phrase is often **give the man/woman a cigar**.

nick 1. To steal something. 2. Condition or state, e.g. 'The car's in pretty good nick'. 3. To be **in the nick** is to be naked. 4. A prison. 5. To capture or arrest. 6. To move with speed, e.g. 'I'll just nick around to the shop'.

nick-and-run A variation of the children's game **hit-and-run** or **tip**.

nick off 1. Go now or get lost, e.g. 'Why don't you just nick off'. 2. To leave in a hurry.

nick out To go out for a short time.

nicky swim In WA, to swim in the nude or skinny-dip.

Nigel An unpopular person, a dag or a nerd. Also known as **Nigel No-friends**.

niggly Angry, bad tempered or on edge, e.g. 'He's been niggly all day'.

the **night's a pup** The night is young.

nightwatchman A lower-order batsman in cricket who is sent in to bat late in the day when the batting team wants to preserve its best batsmen for the next day.

nimby An acronym from Not In My Back Yard and used to describe people who are against having development built near their homes or property.

niner A 9-gallon keg of beer.

nineteenth hole The bar at a golf club.

ning-nong A simple person.

Nip A racist name for a Japanese person.

nipper 1. A young child. 2. A youth on a construction site or in a mine who does small odd jobs. 3. A junior lifesaver.

nippy Cold.

nit 1. A word used to warn people engaged in criminal activity that the police are coming. To **keep nit** is to keep watch. A **nit keeper** keeps watch. 2. A foolish or silly person.

nitwit A foolish or slow-witted person.

nix 1. Nothing, e.g. 'I'd be happy to do it for nix'. 2. Not at all.

Noah's ark 1. Rhyming slang for shark. Also shortened to **Noah's**. 2. Rhyming slang for nark.

no Arthur Murrays Rhyming slang for no worries. Also **no David Murrays**.

nob The head of the penis and, therefore an annoying person or a dickhead. Also a **nob end**.

nob-sucker A contemptible person.

nod 1. Permission to go ahead, e.g. 'I've given him the nod to proceed'. 2. Credit.

nod bet A bet taken on credit.

no flies on you A compliment meaning that you are clever.

noggin 1. The head. 2. A glass of beer, e.g. 'I'm gonna have a couple of noggins with the locals'.

no good to gundy No good at all.

no hoper 1. A person who fails at everything they do or is destitute. 2. A racehorse or greyhound with little promise of succeeding.

nointer In Tasmania, a brat of a child.

no joke This is serious, e.g. 'I'm not very happy, no joke'.

non compos Abbreviation of the Latin phrase *non compos mentis*, which means you are close to unconsciousness due to overindulgence in alcohol.

no-neck A muscular man who is also considered stupid.

nong A silly person or an idiot, e.g. 'You're acting like a real nong'.

no-nuts An effeminate male.

noob Of a boy, new to something.

noodle Your head.

noogie A painful rubbing of the knuckles across someone's head.

nooky Sexual intercourse.

no plum pud Rhyming slang for no good.

no problems Everything is okay and there are no worries. Also shortened to **no probs** and commonly used as **no problemo**.

noras Breasts.

no risk An exclamation of approval or reassurance.

norks Slang term for women's breasts. Also **norgs**.

north and south Rhyming slang for mouth.

the **North Island** In Tasmania, this is a nickname for the mainland.

North Shore Holden Sydney slang for a Volvo.

North Shore tank Sydney slang for a four-wheel-drive used only in the city. Also a **North Shore Kingswood**.

North Snore Sydney's North Shore, noted for its prevalence of conservative people.

nosebag A feed. To **put on the nosebag** is to start a meal.

nosh Food.

noshery A restaurant or café.

no shit Really? Is that true? Commonly used in a sarcastic manner when someone has stated the obvious.

no-show Someone who fails to turn up.

no show without Punch 1. Used to indicate that the most important guest was not present. 2. Also used to have a shot at someone who always needs to be the centre of attention.

nosh-up A meal.

no spring chicken No longer a young person.

nosy parker A stickybeak or someone who continually pries.

not a sausage Absolutely nothing.

not bat an eyelid To be totally unconcerned at what is going on.

not give a rat's arse To not care at all. Also **not give a shit**.

not have a bar Having nothing to do with someone or something, e.g. 'I'm not having a bar of him anymore'.

not in the hunt Not in contention at all.

not know from a bar of soap To be totally unfamiliar with.

not know shit To know nothing at all.

not much chop No good at all.

not on your nelly Absolutely not.

not playing for sheep stations A game that is not as important as some would make out.

not the full quid Someone who is stupid or a bit silly. Also **not the sharpest tool in the shed**.

not worth a cracker To be worth little or nothing. Also **not worth a bumper**, **not worth a crumpet**, **not worth a Mintie**, **not worth a pinch of salt**, **not worth a brass razoo**, **not worth a two bob**, **not worth a zack**, or **not worth the paper it's written on**.

nous Intelligence, e.g. 'he's got plenty of nous'.

no way Jose Under no circumstances.

no work in Bourke Nothing to do or no jobs.

no worries 1. No problems, e.g. 'I'll do it, no worries'. 2. Don't mention it.

no wucking furries A spoonerism of no fucking worries, Also **no wuckers** or **no wucks**.

nude nut A bald person.

nuddy Naked.

nudge the turps To drink alcohol excessively.

nuff 1. Cool or terrific. 2. In Victoria an annoying person. Also a **nuffy**.

nugget 1. A lump of gold. 2. A short muscular man or animal, also said to be **nuggety**. 3. An unbranded calf. 4. A hard blob of excrement.

nuggets 1. Testicles. 2. Excrement.

nuke 1. A nuclear weapon, hence to destroy something is to **nuke it**. 2. To cook in a microwave oven.

number ones To urinate.

number twos To defecate.

numb nuts 1. A gutless man. 2. A fool.

numbskull A dimwitted person.

numero uno 1. The leader or most important person. 2. Oneself, e.g. 'You've gotta look after numero uno'.

nurries The testicles. This term is mainly used in WA.

nut 1. A foolish or insane person. 2. An enthusiast in any field, e.g. 'He was a real model aeroplane nut'. 3. A testicle. 4. The head. To be **off your nut** is to be crazy or deranged. To **do your nut** is to get angry.

nut bag or **nut bar** A fool or crazy person.

nut case A foolish or eccentric person.

nut chokers Men's underwear.

nut house A psychiatric hospital.

nut out To work out or solve something.

nuts 1. Crazy, e.g. 'He's nuts about soccer'. 2. The testicles. To do your nuts over someone is to be infatuated with them. 3. An expression of disgust or disbelief, e.g. 'Nuts to you'.

nutso Crazy.

nutty Silly or stupid.

nutty as a fruitcake To be insane or completely mad.

nylon disgusters Speedos, or men's swimming briefs.

O

ocker Once referred to the archetypal uncultivated and uncultured Australian male but now refers to anything that is typically Australian.

ockerdom The state of 'ockerness', or possessing ocker qualities.

ockerina The female counterpart of the ocker.

ockie An octopus.

ockie strap Shortened version of an octopus strap that is used to tie down loads on the top or back of a vehicle.

odd bod An eccentric person or someone with a particular fixation.

odds on Certain, e.g. 'It's odds on that he's down at the boozer'.

off Disgusting. This is especially used by young people.

offa To be off your head on alcohol or drugs.

offal box A meat pie.

office bike A derogatory term for a woman who has sex with different men in her workplace.

off like a bride's nightie To leave quickly.

off like a bucket of prawns in the midday sun 1. Rotten or stinking. 2. Also to leave quickly, as in to be off quickly.

off the beaten track To be out of the way or uncommon.

off the rails To be mentally unsound, or not in touch with reality. Also **off the air** and **off the planet**.

off with the fairies To be daydreaming or to be mentally unsound. Also **off with the pixies**.

off your face To be really drunk or stoned.

oi or **oy** A cry to attract attention or to warn someone that they shouldn't be doing what they are doing.

oil Information or news, e.g. 'Can you give me the oil on that?' It is generally qualified as in **good oil**, **inside oil**, **dinkum oil** and **straight oil**.

oiled Drunk.

oil the tonsils To drink booze. Also **oil the larynx**.

oinker 1. A pig. 2. An ugly person.

okay or **OK** Correct or all right. Can be used in many ways — as an adverb as in 'She can manage it okay', as a noun as in 'I was given the okay', as a verb to allow or endorse as in 'The boss okayed my leave application', and as a positive answer to a request. Also **okey-doke** and **okey-dokey**.

old bastard A genial address among males, e.g. 'How ya goin', you old bastard?'

old bat An unpleasant old woman.

old bloke 1. Your father. 2. The penis.

old boy 1. Your father. 2. Your husband. 3. Your boss. 4. The penis. 5. Captain of a vessel.

old cheese Your wife. From cheese and kisses, rhyming slang for missus.

old chum A person who had spent some time in the colony, especially in the outback, and was accustomed to Australian life, as opposed to a new chum.

the **Old Country** Generally England or Britain.

the **Old Dart** England.

old fart Any old person.

old fellow 1. Your father. 2. The penis.

old folks Your parents.

old girl 1. Your wife. 2. Your mother.

oldie 1. An elderly person or an old thing. 2. The **oldies** are your parents, e.g. 'I think I'll go visit the oldies this weekend'. Also the **olds**.

old lady 1. Your mother. 2. Your wife.

old lag An ex-convict or ex-prisoner.

old man 1. Your father. 2. Your husband. 3. Your boss. 4. The penis. 5. Captain of a vessel. 6. A large male kangaroo.

old man kangaroo An adult male kangaroo.

old mate A genial term of address to a man, usually by another man. Often used after a man's name as an encouragement.

old timer's disease A jocular alteration of Alzheimer's disease.

old woman 1. Your mother. 2. Your wife. 3. A fussy, silly person of either sex.

on 1. To have placed a bet. 2. To have started, e.g. 'It was on for young and old'. 3. Willing to take part in something.

on a good wicket To be in a great position, or poised for success.

on a promise Of a man who has been promised sexual intercourse, e.g. 'I'll give it a miss, I'm on a promise'.

once-over To give a cursory perusal of something.

oncer Something that is done or made just once.

one-armed bandit A poker machine.

one-dog night A night that is a little chilly with only one dog needed to keep a bushman warm.

one-eyed trouser snake The penis.

one for Ron Something that is borrowed for later on.

one-handed reading Pornographic material.

one out To do something by yourself.

one-pub town A small country town with one pub.

onesies A child's term for urination.

on for young and old A commotion involving everyone.

onkaparinga Rhyming slang for finger. Shortened to **onka** or **onker**.

on the battle Working as a prostitute.

on the blink Something that is not working properly and about to break down completely.

on the boil 1. Doing something without pausing. 2. In football to be running at full speed. Also **on the burst**.

on the bugle Something that is very smelly.

on the dole Someone who is receiving social security benefits for being unemployed.

on the game Working as a prostitute.

on the improve Something that is improving.

on the land To be working as a farmer.

on the make 1. Looking for a sexual partner. 2. Intent on personal gain.

on the money Correct, e.g. 'He was right on the money'.

on the Murray cod Rhyming slang for on the nod, or on credit.

on the never-never Something that is on hire purchase.

on the nod A bet taken on credit.

on the nose 1. Smelly. 2. Unpleasant.

on the outer Someone who has been ostracised.

on the QT On the quiet.

on the scoot On a drinking binge.

on the square 1. To be living an honest life. 2. In a faithful relationship with someone.

on the take To be in receipt of bribes.

on the tit A baby who is being breastfed.

on the toe 1. To flee. 2. Nervous.

on the track To travel as a swagman. Also **on the wallaby track**.

on the trot 1. In succession, e.g. 'The champion won six races on the trot'. 2. Continuous activity.

on with Romantically involved with someone.

onya Well done. Abbreviation of 'good on you'.

on your hammer To be followed closely or tailgated.

on your lonesome To be all alone. Also **on your Pat Malone**, rhyming slang for on your own.

oodles A large quantity.

Oodnawoopwoop An imaginary remote town. Also **Oodnagalahbi**.

oo-er An exclamation of pretended shock.

oo-roo Good bye. Also **hooroo**.

op 1. A surgical operation, e.g. 'Harry's goin' in for his op tomorrow'. 2. A military operation. 3. An operator.

open go A free chance.

open slather To go all out with no restraints.

op shop An opportunity shop where second-hand clothes and goods are sold to raise funds for charity. They are known elsewhere in the world as a charity shop.

optic An eye.

optic nerve Rhyming slang for perve, or to look lustily at the opposite sex. Also **optic**.

orchestras Short for orchestra stalls, which is rhyming slang for balls or testicles.

order of the boot To be given this is to be fired from your job.

ordinary Nothing special.

Orstralia Australians taking off the English when they say Australia.

ort Slang for the anus. Origin unknown but first recorded in 1952, e.g. 'Stick that in your ort, mate'.

oscar Short for Oscar Asche, which is rhyming slang for cash.

OS Overseas.

out 1. To publicly expose someone as gay or lesbian. 2. To reveal on impostor. 3. To suspend someone from playing a sport. 4. To dismiss or sack. 5. A **run of outs** is a succession of bad luck.

outback Any remote part of Australia.

outer An open betting place at a racecourse. Also the area around the ring in two-up where gamblers gather. To be **on the outer** is to be excluded.

out-gun To defeat convincingly.

outie A protruding belly button, as opposed to an 'innie'.

outlaw A horse that is difficult to handle.

outlaws A jocular term for your in-laws.

out of whack In disorder or not functioning properly.

outside Prison slang for the world outside prison.

outta here To leave.

over-the-shoulder-boulder-holder A jocular term for a bra.

ow-ya-goin'? Typically Aussie way of asking about someone's wellbeing.

Oxford scholar Rhyming slang for dollar.

oxygen thief A useless human being who is wasting oxygen by breathing.

Oz Australian. Also **Ozzie.**

P

pack a wallop To have a strong impact.

packed lunch The male genitalia as seen through clothing.

packing To be very scared. Also **packing shit**, **packing death** or **packing darkies**.

pack of galahs A group of idiots or disliked people.

pack of poo tickets 1. Something that is in a terrible mess. 2. A roll of toilet paper.

Paddo The Sydney or Brisbane suburbs of Paddington.

paddock 1. A sporting field and commonly used in Aussie Rules. 2. An enclosure for spectators at a racecourse.

paddock basher or **paddock bomb** An old car, generally unregistered, used for driving around the paddocks or the bush.

paddock chicken A wild rabbit.

Paddy's lantern The moon.

Paddy's poke A cut made in a deck of cards by poking out the middle section with a finger and placing those cards on top.

paddy wagon A police vehicle for transporting people who have been arrested.

paddywhack Rhyming slang for back.

paddywhacking To spank someone.

pain in the arse Someone or something that is annoying or disagreeable.

pair Getting out for a duck in both innings of a cricket match.

pakapoo ticket Something that is a terrible mess, especially written work. It originally referred to the tickets used in a Chinese gambling game that were marked with Chinese characters, which to western eyes looked like messy scribble.

pal A good friend or buddy. To **pal up** is to become someone's friend.

palooka A hopeless boxer but also used to describe any big, stupid man.

palsy-walsy Very friendly.

panic merchant Someone who is always panicking or worrying.

pan licker A dog. Also a **dish licker**.

panno A panel van.

pansy Derisive term for an effeminate male or a gay man.

pants To pull someone's pants down as a joke. Also **dack**.

pants man Someone who fancies himself as a bit of a womaniser.

paper Aussie A naturalised Australian citizen.

paper bag job A phrase describing someone who is so ugly that you'd have to put a paper bag over their head when having sex with them.

papers Cigarette papers. In Tasmania they are called **tissues**.

para Very drunk. Short for **paralytic**.

park a tiger To vomit.

parkie 1. Someone who sleeps in a city park. 2. A parking inspector. 3. A park ranger.

parking Kissing, fondling and other amorous activities carried out while in a parked car.

park the carcass To take a seat.

party animal Someone who enjoys parties and parties hard while there.

party pooper A spoil sport.

pash 1. A long passionate kiss. 2. A session of passionate kissing. 3. To kiss passionately. **Pash on** is to have a prolonged kissing session and **pash off** is to kiss someone until fully satisfied.

pash rash A reddened face from excessive kissing.

pass in your marbles To die.

passion wagon A panel van used as a place for sexual encounters.

pass the buck To give a task to somebody else or to pass on something difficult.

pasting A thorough beating, e.g. 'The team copped a real pasting today'.

Pat Malone Rhyming slang for on your own. Also shortened to **pat** as in **on your pat**.

pav Short for **pavlova**, the great Aussie dessert.

pavement pizza Dried vomit left on the footpath.

pay out To criticise someone is to **give them a payout** or **pay them out**.

pay your dues To earn your place in a line-up.

pea A favourite or certainty in a horse race.

peabrain A fool or an idiot.

pea floater A meat pie served floating in pea soup.

peak 1. To reach a pinnacle of enjoyment. 2. To climax sexually. 3. To reach the greatest height of a wave.

peanut 1. A fool or idiot. 2. A small penis.

pearler Wonderful or excellent. A real beauty, e.g. 'Her new dress was a real pearler'.

pearlies The teeth. Also **pearly whites**.

pearl necklace Sperm ejaculated on the chest of a sexual partner. Also **string of pearls**.

pear-shaped A description of something that has gone awry, e.g. 'That job's gone pear-shaped'.

peasants The term older school students use to refer to young students.

pea soup A thick fog. Also **pea souper**.

pedal to the metal To drive a vehicle at top speed.

pee To urinate.

peel To take your clothes off.

peewee The common small black and white bird known officially as the magpie lark. It has a loud piping voice that sounds like it is calling 'peewee, peewee'. Also called **mud lark** in Victoria and WA, and **Murray magpie** in SA.

peg 1. To throw or toss something. 2. To look or peep. 3. To observe someone and comprehend their true nature, e.g. 'He's got you pegged'.

peg leg To jump into water with one leg tucked under your arms and pulled into the chest and the other extended straight out. Also called a **banana**, **can opener** or **horsey**.

peg out To die.

pelican A fool.

pelt Red hair.

pen and ink Rhyming slang for drink.

pencil To work as a bookmaker's clerk. The role is called a **penciller**.

pencil neck A geek with a thin neck.

penguin A nun.

penguin suit A dinner suit.

Percy The penis. Often heard in the phrase **point Percy at the porcelain**, which refers to male urination.

perform To throw a tantrum or to make a fuss. A person who habitually does this is called a **performer**.

performer An energetic lover.

perk 1. An extra advantage or fringe benefit obtained at work or in an official capacity apart from wages. 2. To throw up or vomit.

persuader A whip or crop used by a jockey.

perve or **perv** 1. To look lustily at an attractive person. 2. A sexual pervert. 3. An attractive person or one who is worth perving on. 4. To look at but not in a sexual way.

pester To annoy or bother someone, e.g. 'I wish she'd stop pestering me'.

peter 1. A prison cell. 2. The till of a cash register. To **tickle the peter** is to steal from the till while using it. 3. The penis.

peter thief A jail inmate who steals from other cells.

petrol bowsers Rhyming slang for trousers.

petrol head A car enthusiast.

pew A reference to any chair or a place where one can sit down, e.g. 'Why don't you take a pew?'

PGB A Post-grog Bog.

phlegm cake A vanilla slice. Also a **phlegm sandwich**.

phwoar An exclamation expressing appreciation of an attractive person.

physio Short for physiotherapist or physiotherapy.

piano arms The flabby triceps of an overweight or matronly woman.

Piccadilly Rhyming slang for chilly.

piccaninny An Aboriginal child.

piccaninny daylight The first light of day.

piccy A photograph or illustration.

pick To start a fight with someone.

pick a winner To pick a large piece of snot from the nose.

pickled Drunk.

picnic 1. Something that is very easy, e.g. 'This exam was a picnic'. 2. Aussie sarcasm for something unpleasant.

piddle To urinate.

piddle about or **piddle around** To fiddle about achieving little.

piece 1. A woman seen as a sex object. 2. A sandwich. 3. To **take a piece out of** someone is to chastise them.

piece of piss A very easy task, e.g. 'This job's a piece of piss'. Also **piece of piss to a trained digger**.

piece of skirt A woman viewed as a sexual object.

pie-eater Someone of little importance.

pie-eyed Drunk.

piff A Victorian slang term to throw.

pig 1. A person with attributes like a pig, such as eating too much, being messy or not sharing. 2. A derogatory term for a police officer.

pig dog A bull terrier or a dog used for hunting wild pigs.

pigging The hunting of wild pigs with dogs.

pig ignorant Very ignorant.

Pig Iron Bob A nickname of former Prime Minister Sir Robert Menzies. This arose from his selling of pig iron to Japan while Minister for Industry before World War II.

pig out To eat a lot of food like a pig, or a meal at which there is excessive eating.

pig's arse Strong disagreement or bullshit. Also **pig's tit**, **pig's bum**, **pig's ear** or just **pig's**.

pig's ear Rhyming slang for beer.

pike 1. To **pike on** someone is to let them down. 2. To **pike out** is to fail to contribute a fair share to a team effort or to go back on an arrangement.

piker 1. Someone who chickens out of doing something or fails to contribute. Also a person who lets you down at the last minute. 2. A timid gambler.

pile driver A powerful punch or kick.

pile it on To exaggerate.

pill The football in Aussie Rules or rugby.

Pilliga yowie A yowie said to inhabit the Pilliga area of northern central NSW.

pillow Someone who is a wimp, especially in sport.

pillow hair Messy hair caused by sleeping.

pimp Someone who tells tales on you.

pimples A derogatory term for small breasts.

pinch 1. To steal. 2. To arrest. 3. A steep hill or sudden rise.

pin dick 1. A male with a small penis. 2. Someone of little intelligence.

pineapple A $50 note.

ping 1. To penalise for an infringement. 2. A sudden burst of speed by a racehorse.

ping off A euphemism for piss off and often used by children.

pin head A silly person.

pink bits The female genitalia.

pink fit A tantrum or a burst of anger. If you wouldn't do something **in a pink fit** then you would never do it.

pinkie In Victoria, a parking ticket.

pinko A communist or leftist sympathiser.

pinnies Pinball machines.

pins The legs.

pip If someone **gives you the pip** they are causing you extreme annoyance.

pipe opener 1. An alcoholic drink consumed early in the day, often as a hangover remedy. 2. Any drink consumed early in the day.

pipes The respiratory passages.

pipsqueak A small or insignificant person.

piss 1. Urine or to urinate. If you have a low regard for someone you **wouldn't piss on them** or you **wouldn't piss on them if they were on fire**. Contempt can also be expressed by saying you **wouldn't piss in their ear if their brain was on fire**. An insignificant amount of something is called a **piss in the ocean**. 2. Alcohol. To be **on the piss** is to be on a binge. 3. To **take the piss out of** someone is to make fun of them. 4. Also used as an intensifier in front of other words, such as piss-awful or piss-poor. It can also be substituted for hell, as in 'I had the piss scared out of me'.

piss about To mess around.

piss along To move quickly.

piss and wind Something or someone with little or no substance, e.g. 'That bloke's all piss and wind'.

pissant 1. An annoying little bastard. 2. To be **drunk as a pissant** is to be very drunk. 3. Small and insignificant.

pissant around To waste time.

piss artist A drunkard or a good drinker.

piss away If you **piss something away** you squander it. Also to **piss it up against the wall**.

piss bolt To run at great speed.

piss cake A urinal disinfectant lozenge.

piss down To rain heavily.

piss-easy Very easy.

pissed 1. Really drunk. Also **pissed as a parrot**, **pissed as a fart**, **pissed as a bastard**, **pissed as a newt**, **pissed as an owl**, **pissed as forty arseholes** and **pissed to the eyeballs**. 2. Extremely annoyed or in a bad mood.

pissed off Angry or upset with someone or something.

piss-elegant Pretensions to elegance.

pisser 1. Something that is very funny. 2. A urinal. 3. The pub. 4. Something bad or a bad outcome.

piss-fart To waste time.

piss fat A morning erection caused by having a full bladder. Also a **piss horn**.

piss head A heavy drinker.

piss house A toilet.

to **piss in someone's pocket** To flatter someone.

piss into the wind To waste time striving for something that can't be done.

piss it in To win easily, e.g. 'The greyhound has pissed it in'.

piss take To play a joke on someone or to criticise them.

piss off 1. To leave or depart quickly. 2. A command to get lost. 3. To be rid of someone. 4. To annoy someone.

piss on 1. To beat comprehensively. Also to **piss all over**. 2. A party or function involving drinking.

piss-poor Third rate.

pisspot 1. A heavy drinker. 2. A chamber pot.

piss-take A satirical version.

piss-up A drinking session.

piss-weak 1. Mean or despicable. 2. Cowardly.

pissy 1. Wet with urine. 2. A little drunk. 3. Irritable. 4. Something that is insignificant.

piss yourself 1. To be very fearful. 2. To laugh loudly and heartily.

pits An unpleasant place.

Pitt Street Refers to any busy place, e.g. 'It's like Pitt Street down here'. Derived from one of Sydney's busiest streets.

Pitt Street farmer In NSW, a person who lives in the city and owns a country property often for tax avoidance purposes.

pizza face Someone with a bad case of acne.

pizzling A heavy defeat, e.g. 'We copped a real pizzling last weekend'.

plastered Drunk.

plastic A credit or ATM card or the cards collectively.

plates of meat Rhyming slang for feet.

play funny buggers or **play silly buggers** To mess around, e.g. 'Don't play funny buggers with me'.

playing like a second-hand whipper-snipper Not playing well at all.

playing possum Pretending to be asleep.

pleased as Punch Delighted.

pleb A common or ordinary person; a shortened form of plebeian.

plod card A time sheet.

plodder A slow, but steady worker who eventually gets the job done.

plonk 1. Cheap wine or some use this term to refer to any wine. 2. A large amount of money bet on a horse.

plonk artist An immoderate wine drinker.

plonko An alcoholic who drinks wine.

plonk shop A bottle shop.

pluggers Thongs with only one plug under the foot.

plug-ugly Very unattractive.

plum Something or someone that is exceptional.

plumber's smile The portion of a buttock cleft that shows above the top of the pants. Also **plumber's crack** or **plumber's bike rack**.

plunge 1. A large sum of money wagered on a horse or greyhound. 2. In Queensland, a bath.

plunger Someone who bets large amounts on the races.

pluto pup A battered sausage on a stick. Also called a **dagwood dog** or a **dippy dog**.

po A chamber pot or potty. Although they are seldom used these days the word persists in the phrase **full as a family po**, which means completely full, and in the insult **po-faced**.

poached egg A traffic dome or silent cop. Also called a **fried egg**.

pocket billiards A male playing with his genitals while his hands are in his pockets. Also called **pocket pool**.

poddy 1. A young calf, especially one that is not branded. 2. A calf, lamb or foal that has been handfed.

poddy-dodge The theft of unbranded cattle.

podies Girls who think they are popular but are not. Also used of girls who are 'plastic' or fake.

poet's day An Aussie term for Friday. This is an acronym for Piss Off Early Tomorrow's Saturday.

pogo stick Rhyming slang for prick.

point Percy at the porcelain Of a male, to urinate into a toilet bowl.

point the bone To indicate a person who is guilty. Also **point the finger**.

poisoner A cook, especially a shearers' cook.

poke 1. To have sex with someone. 2. The penis. 3. A street name for Viagra when used as a sexual stimulant.

poke borak at To make fun of someone. Also **poke mullock at**.

pokies Poker machines.

pole on To bludge on others. Someone who is good at this is a **poler**.

poley cup A cup that has lost its handle. Poley is a rural term for hornless cattle.

pollie Slang for a politician.

Pollyanna A girl with her hair up in the front and loose at the back.

pollywaffle Floating human excrement. So called after the chocolate bar it resembles.

Pom or **Pommy** An English person. The term is considered by some English as being derogatory. There are various explanations for the origins of the word and one of the most common is that it stands for Prisoner of Mother England but this is unlikely as acronyms were not used before the 1950s and transportation had ceased 75 years before the term first appeared. The likely source is pomegranate, which is rhyming slang for immigrant.

pommy bastard An English person who is the antithesis of all things Australian.

Pommyland England.

ponce 1. A derogatory term for a gay man and used to describe any man considered to be lacking in masculinity. Also **poncy**. 2. A pimp.

ponce about To flounce about in an effeminate manner.

pong A bad smell, e.g. 'Where's that pong coming from?'

pony In WA, a beer glass of 5 fluid ounces. Sometimes also used for a 4 ounce glass.

poo Excrement or to excrete. Often substituted in other phrases instead of the word shit, including **in the poo** and to **have the poos**.

poo-brown An unattractive brown colour.

poo bum or **poo head** An annoying person.

poof or **poofter** A derogatory term for a male homosexual.

poofter bashing The assaulting of homosexual men by certain homophobic men, often in groups.

poofter shot A shot in pool, snooker or billiards played with the rest and seen as being gutless. The rest is called a **poofter stick**.

poon A fool or a dill.

poonce A derogatory term for a homosexual man and also used to describe any man considered to be lacking in masculinity.

pooned up Dressed up to go out.

poontang A crass term for the vagina and, therefore sexual intercourse.

poop Excrement or to excrete. To be **in the poop** is to be in trouble.

poop cart A horse-drawn cart used to collect dunny cans. Also a **dunny cart**.

poota or **puter** A shortening of computer.

pop off To pass wind.

poppycock Nonsense or rubbish.

popular To be **as popular as a cross-city tunnel** is to not be popular at all. Also **as popular as a paparazzo at a Tom Cruise wedding**.

POQ A polite way of saying 'Piss off quickly'.

porcupine An alternate name for the echidna and mainly used in Tasmania.

pork Of a male, to have sex.

pork and bean Rhyming slang for queen, or a homosexual male.

pork chop 1. To be **silly as a pork chop** is to be really silly. Also to **carry on like a pork chop**. 2. An unwanted object or person is said to be **like a pork chop at a Jewish wedding.**

porker 1. A pig. 2. A fat person.

porkie Short for **pork pie**, which is rhyming slang for lie.

port A suitcase or school bag. This use is peculiar to Queensland as well as the north coast and inland areas of NSW.

portergaff A drink of stout with a dash of lemonade.

possie or **pozzie** A place or position, e.g. 'I'll get us a good possie near the fence'.

possum 1. An affectionate term of address, e.g. 'How are you going, possum?' 2. To **stir the possum** is to create a disturbance. 3. A victim of a swindle or con trick.

poster In Aussie Rules a kick which hits one of the four goal posts.

postie A postman.

pot 1. In Victoria, Tasmania and Queensland a 285ml or 10 fluid ounce beer glass. Also called a **middy** or **ten**. 2. Marijuana. 3. A heavily backed horse. Also **hot pot**.

pot and pan Rhyming slang for man.

potato 1. A woman or girl. Short for potato peeler, which is rhyming slang for sheila. 2. A small hole in a sock through which skin is showing.

pothead A marijuana user.

pothole Someone who is always in the road.

poultice A large bet or any large sum of money.

pov 1. Shortening of poverty, hence a poor person. 2. Used mainly by young people and meaning bad or uncool. Also **povvo** or **povvy**.

pov cone An inexpensive McDonald's ice-cream cone that even povs can afford.

powder puff An effeminate male.

powder your nose 1. A euphemism used by a woman when wanting to visit the toilet or ladies' room. 2. Referring to the snorting of cocaine.

pox doctor A doctor treating venereal disease.

poxhead A contemptible person.

poxy No good or rubbish.

prairie oyster A testicle of a castrated bull or ram that is eaten as food. Also **mountain oyster**.

prang To crash a car, bike or other vehicle. Also the result of such a crash.

prat 1. A fool or jerk. 2. The arse.

prat fall A heavy fall onto the buttocks.

prat yourself in To intrude.

prawn 1. A shrimp. 2. A fool, jerk or an insignificant person. Also a **prawn head**. If someone **comes the raw prawn** with you they are trying to deceive you or dupe you. 3. Someone with an attractive body but an ugly head. 4. To be **off like a bucket of prawns** is to be rotten.

preggers Pregnant. Also **preggo** or **preggie**.

pregnant rollerskate The original Volkswagen Beetle.

Presbo A Presbyterian.

pretty To an extent, e.g. 'Looks pretty good to me'.

pretty much or **pretty well**. Almost completely, e.g. 'It's pretty well stuffed'.

prezzies or **pressies** Gifts or presents.

prick 1. The penis. 2. A contemptible person. Also **prick features** and **prick nose**.

prickle farmer An urban resident who takes up farming a small block of land in a rural area.

prickteaser A woman or girl who leads a man on but doesn't come across. Also **cockteaser**.

pro 1. A prostitute. 2. A professional. 3. A problem.

prob Short for problem, e.g. 'What's the prob?' Also used in the reply **no probs**.

Proddie or **Protto**. A Protestant. Also a **Proddy dog**.

professional ratbag A conman or someone who is not to be trusted.

projector bitch A girl who always sits at the front of the class and operates the technology.

prole A member of the proletariat or working class.

prong An erect penis.

pronto Quickly or promptly.

psyche To go mental or crazy. Also **psyche out**.

psycho 1. Crazy or insane, e.g. 'Look out, that bloke's gone psycho'. 2. An insane person.

pubbo A kid who attends a public school.

pub crawl Calling in to one hotel bar after another until you are totally inebriated.

pube 1. A pubic hair. 2. Derogatory term for a public servant.

pub golf A pub crawl on which nine pubs are visited with each one having a certain 'par' of how many beers are to be sunk.

pug hole A hole in a dried-up waterhole.

puke To vomit.

pull 1. A jockey preventing a horse from running on its merits. Also **pull up**. 2. To successfully get someone to have sex with you. 3. A male masturbating.

pull a chick To woo a woman into bed.

pull a fastie To deceive someone.

pull off 1. To achieve something. 2. Of a male, to masturbate.

pull on the wobbly boot To prepare to go out and get drunk. Someone who is drunk is said to have **pulled on the wobbly boot**.

pull your finger out To get on with the job.

pull your head in Telling someone to mind their own business or not to make outrageous statements.

pull your pud Of a male, to masturbate.

pump To have sexual intercourse.

pumpie A pump-action shotgun.

punch buggy A children's game in which punches are dealt out to others on sighting a Volkswagen Beetle.

punch-drunk Describes someone suffering cerebral damage after having been hit in the head many times or involved in many fights or boxing matches. Also **punchy**.

punt 1. To have a bet. 2. Gambling in general, e.g. 'He could make a living on the punt'.

punter 1. Someone who bets on the races. 2. A customer or the person who is paying for something.

punter's eyes Someone whose eyes are a little wonky and seem to be looking in different directions, i.e. one each way.

purse carrier Derogatory term for a homosexual man.

pus ball A pimple.

pus face Someone badly affected with acne.

pushie A pushbike.

push shit uphill with a pointy stick To attempt something that is impossible.

pus pie A vanilla slice or a custard tart.

pussy 1. The vagina. 2. Used to refer to women considered as sexual objects. 3. Sexual intercourse. 4. An ineffectual man or a wimp. 5. A sook.

pussyfoot around Trying hard not to offend and thereby taking very cautious steps.

pussy-whipped A man who is dominated by his wife or a female partner. He is also said to be **under the thumb**.

put a cork in it Shut up.

put in the fangs To borrow from someone. Also **put in the hooks**.

put lead in your pencil To sexually excite a man.

put one over An attempt to deceive.

putrid Used mainly by young people for excellent or cool.

put some wood in the hole Close the door.

put the acid on To pressure someone into doing something they don't want to do.

put the boot in 1. To attack savagely by kicking. 2. To attack unfairly without restraint.

put the hard word on 1. To be persistent in asking for a favour. 2. To pursue sexual favours.

put the mocker on To bring bad luck to someone.

put the scarers on To frighten someone.

put the shits up To alarm someone.

put the wind up Urging someone to do something, e.g. 'I had to put the wind up him'.

put-up A pre-meditated deed planned in a devious manner.

put up or shut up To support what someone says or remain silent.

pyjama game One-day cricket. So called because coloured uniforms are worn rather than traditional white.

pyro Short for pyromaniac.

Q

quack A doctor, e.g. 'She's gone to see the quack'.

quacker Nickname for a Kawasaki motorcycle.

quad 1. A quadrangle or courtyard. 2. A four-wheeled rail motor. 3. A four-wheeled motorcycle.

Quaint Arse A nickname for QANTAS.

quandong Someone who cadges or imposes upon another.

queen An effeminate male homosexual.

Queenslander A weatherboard house built well above the ground and common in Queensland.

Queen Street bushie In Queensland, this is someone who owns a country property, often of only a few hectares, for tax avoidance purposes. Also a **Queen Street ringer**.

queeny Effeminate.

queer A homosexual male.

queer for Infatuated with someone.

Queer Street To be in a state of financial embarrassment.

quiche-eater A derisive term for a man who is sensitive, kind and has new-age principles.

quickie 1. Sexual intercourse on the fly. 2. A quick drink. 3. Anything done rapidly.

quick quid A small amount of money earned with minimal effort.

quid 1. A pound but still used today to indicate any form of money. To **make a quid** is to earn a living. 2. To be **not the full quid** is to be lacking in intelligence. 3. If you won't do something **for quids** then you won't do it under any circumstances. 4. If you desperately want to see something then you **wouldn't miss it for quids**. 5. The great Aussie expression of the will to enjoy life is **I wouldn't be dead for quids**.

quiet one or a **quietie** To have a quiet drink.

quim The female genitalia.

quince 1. A homosexual man. 2. To **get on someone's quince** is to annoy or irritate them.

quod Prison or jail.

quoit The anus or backside. Also spelt **coit**.

R

rabbit 1. A fool or silly person. 2. A cricket player who is not very good at batting. Also a **bunny**. 3. To **root like rabbits** is to indulge enthusiastically in sex.

rabbit ears An indoor television aerial with two adjustable arms.

rabbit on To talk incessantly.

racehorse 1. A cigarette or joint that has been rolled thinly and is smoked quickly. 2. In WA, a sand goanna.

race off To **race someone off** is to take them to a secluded place for sex.

racers Speedos.

racing chook In Tasmania, the flightless native hen. Also a **narkie**.

rack 1. A pair of large breasts. 2. Among teenagers, a French kiss. 3. To rob or steal.

racket 1. A dishonest scheme or a swindle. 2. Legitimate business or an occupation, e.g. 'He's in the car sales racket'.

rack off Go away, scram or get lost. Also **rack off hairy legs**.

radical Great or fantastic. Also **rad**.

Rafferty's rules No rules whatsoever.

rag 1. A newspaper of little substance or quality. Also used to describe any local newspaper. 2. A derogatory term for a woman, implying she is promiscuous. 3. A woman **on her rags** is menstruating.

rage To party. A person who parties hard is a **rager**.

rag trade The clothing industry.

rails The railings around the track at a racecourse. It is also the part of the ground for spectators next to the rails where the leading bookmakers, or **rails bookies**, are set up as opposed to others on the **flat**.

railway tracks Braces worn on the teeth.

rainbow dozen A mixed dozen of the range of Cascade beers, i.e. blue, red and green.

raincoat A euphemism for a condom.

rainmaker A very high kick in Aussie Rules. The high bombs in rugby league or up and unders in rugby union are also sometimes called rainmakers.

rake A comb.

rake-off A share of a profit.

ralph To vomit. So called because the word imitates the sound of vomiting.

ram 1. A highly sexed male. 2. A swindler's accomplice.

Rambo An aggressive, macho male character.

rammies Pants. An alteration of 'round mes', short for 'round me houses', rhyming slang for trousers.

rancid Used by young people for cool or excellent.

random 1. A non-local or outsider. 2. A word used by young people for almost any collection or group.

rap 1. A favourable appraisal or a compliment. 2. A review. 3. Blame or punishment. 4. A criminal charge.

rapt To be infatuated with someone or something.

rare as hen's teeth Something that is very rare or scarce.

raspberry A sound made by blowing sloppily with the tongue stuck out through the lips. It is also the sound made by blowing sloppily with the lips on someone's skin.

raspberry tart Rhyming slang for fart.

rat 1. A contemptible person. 2. A person who betrays or informs on others. 3. A chihuahua dog. 4. To desert someone when they are in trouble. 5. To continue at work during a strike. 6. To pike out. 7. To rob or steal from. 8. In Tasmania, an undersized crayfish.

ratbag 1. An untrustworthy, despicable or worthless person, e.g. 'That bloke's a real ratbag'. 2. An eccentric person.

rat cunning Shrewd or sly.

rat house A psychiatric hospital.

rat on stilts A racing greyhound. Also **dish licker**.

rat's arse If you **don't give a rat's arse** you don't care at all.

rat's carcase or **rat's coffin** A meat pie.

ratshit Feeling bad or of inferior quality.

rat's tail A single, long thin lock of hair that is often plaited.

rats with wings The feral pigeons that inhabit many towns and cities.

rat tamer A psychiatrist or a psychologist.

rat through To rifle through things hurriedly.

rattletrap An old car that rattles a lot.

rattler Various trains noted for their rattling. They are usually older trains. To **jump a rattler** was to board a moving train without having a ticket.

rattle your dags Hurry up or get a move one.

ratty Eccentric or crazy.

raw prawn Someone who is naïve and foolish. To **act the raw prawn** is to pretend to be ignorant.

razoo A fictional coin of little value. If you **haven't got a brass razoo** you are stone broke.

razz To make fun of someone.

Razzle or **Razza** An RSL club.

readies Ready cash.

reality check Bringing oneself back down to earth.

reccy To survey an area for a film or to check out an area to become familiar with it.

rec grounds Town recreation grounds or footy ovals.

reckon To estimate, e.g. 'I reckon we'll be there in an hour'.

recovery party A party held the day after a big event when people can wind down. Also **recovery**.

red 1. A red kangaroo. 2. A communist or leftist sympathiser.

red back A $20 note.

red can A can of Melbourne Bitter beer.

the **Red Centre** The desert interior of Australia.

red handbag A cask of cheap red wine.

red-headed rabbit rooter A title directed at any red-headed bloke.

red-hot 1. Enthusiastic or keen. 2. Unfair, e.g. 'Those prices are a bit red-hot'. 3. Highly sexually arousing. 4. By a long margin, e.g. 'The horse was a red-hot favourite'.

red hots Harness racing. Rhyming slang for the trots.

red light district An area inhabited by prostitutes and where brothels, strip clubs and X-rated bookshops are prevalent.

red ned Cheap red wine, such as that found in flagons.

red nut Someone with red hair.

red ragger A derisive term for a communist or leftist sympathiser.

red rattler An old passenger train with red carriages which rattled a lot when travelling at speed.

red rover A schoolyard chasings game. Also called **red rover cross over** and **British bulldog**.

red sails in the sunset Menstruating.

red suitcase A cask of red wine.

reffo Abbreviation of refugee.

Reg Grundies Rhyming slang for undies.

rego Abbreviation of registration, e.g. 'The rego's due on the car'.

reject A socially unacceptable person.

rellie A relative, e.g. 'The rellies are coming over for a barbie'.

rent boy A young male homosexual prostitute.

rents The parents of someone living at home.

repro A reproduction.

reptile An unscrupulous reporter.

retard An awkward or clumsy person.

retent A meticulous person.

retread Someone who has come out of retirement to work again.

retro 1. Fashion and music tastes of previous decades. 2. Old-fashioned.

reverse biceps Flabby triceps.

rev head A car enthusiast.

rice grinder Derogatory term for a Japanese motorcycle.

Richard If something's **had the Richard**, it's **had the dick** or in other words it is wrecked or useless.

Richard the Third A piece of excrement. Rhyming slang for turd. Also **Henry the Third** and **William the Third**.

riding one, leading one To be drinking a beer and have another waiting for you.

ride To have sexual intercourse with someone.

ride shotgun To sit in the front passenger seat when on a journey.

ridgy-didge 1. A true, genuine article. 2. Rhyming slang for fridge.

righto That's right or okay. Also **righty-oh**.

right stuff Alcohol or booze.

ring 1. An uncomplimentary term for the anus. 2. In two-up it is the circle of punters within which the coins are tossed. 3. The area of a racecourse where most bookmakers congregate. 4. In shearing to **ring the shed** is to beat the other shearers with your tally.

ringdinger A two-stroke motorcycle.

ringer 1. The fastest shearer in the shed. 2. Anyone who is a **dead ringer** looks like someone else, e.g. 'She's a dead ringer for Kylie Minogue'. 3. A stockman or drover. 4. A substitute racehorse or greyhound.

ringie The person running a two-up game. Also a **ring keeper** or **ring master**.

ring in 1. To substitute a racehorse or greyhound for another. 2. Substituting a double-sided coin for a genuine one in two-up.

ring-in 1. An imposter, e.g. 'I reckon that bloke's a ring-in'. 2. A racehorse or greyhound substituted for another in a race. Also refers to a person or thing substituted for another at the last moment. 3. Someone from another place.

ringstinger 1. Anal sex. 2. A homosexual male.

rinsed Drunk.

rip 1. To travel at great speed. 2. To surf, skate, ski or snowboard very well. 3. To be excellent.

rip off To swindle or overcharge.

rip-off A poor deal or something that is more expensive than what it is worth.

ripped Severely affected by alcohol or drugs.

ripper 1. An exclamation expressing delight or excitement. Often used as **you little ripper**. 2. Something that is great, e.g. 'It was a ripper of a party'.

rip-roaring Something loud or tumultuous, e.g. 'We had a rip-roaring booze-up'.

ripsnorter Something or someone that is really great, e.g. 'That car is a real ripsnorter'.

rissole 1. An RSL club. To **do the rissoles** is to tour RSL clubs. 2. **See ya round like a rissole** is goodbye or see you later.

rip the fork out of your nightie Something that is amazing or astounding.

roach 1. A cockroach. 2. The butt of a marijuana cigarette.

roadie 1. A road manager for a rock group or a group of performers. 2. A bottle or can of beer consumed while driving. Also a **traveller**. 3. A measure of distance equivalent to the distance travelled while consuming a bottle or can of beer. 4. To have one final beer before hitting the road. Also **one for the road**.

roaring Something that is doing well, e.g. 'Business is really roaring'.

robber's dog An ugly person is said to have a **head like a robber's dog**.

rock 1. To be very good or excellent, e.g. 'The band really rocks'. 2. To travel to some place, e.g. 'I'm going to rock along later'. 3. To alarm someone with a cutting remark.

the **Rock** Uluru, formerly known as Ayers Rock.

rock and roller A Rolls Royce car.

rock ape 1. A lout or hooligan. 2. A derogatory term for someone with dark skin.

rock box A ghettoblaster.

rock chick A female rock 'n'roll musician.

rock chopper A Roman Catholic.

rock doctor A geologist.

rocket 1. To **cop a rocket** from the boss means you have been reprimanded. 2. To **put a rocket under** someone is to stir them into action.

rocket scientist An intelligent person. If something is **not rocket science** it is easy to comprehend.

rock lobster A $20 note.

rock 'n' roll 1. Rhyming slang for the dole. 2. To begin doing something, e.g. 'Right, let's rock 'n'roll'.

rock spider Slang term for a child molester.

rock up To arrive.

Rocky The Queensland town of Rockhampton.

rod 1. A pistol. 2. An erect penis. To **have the rod** is to be worn out or wrecked.

rod walloper A male who masturbates.

roger 1. Of a man, to have sex with someone. 2. To treat harshly.

rogue A racehorse that is hard to handle.

roids Steroids.

roll 1. To assault and rob someone. 2. To convince someone to become a witness and incriminate others. 3. A bankroll. A big bankroll can be **a roll so big Jack Rice couldn't jump over it**. Jack Rice was a famous hurdles racehorse.

Roller A Rolls Royce car.

rollie A roll-your-own cigarette.

roll over To incriminate others after initially claiming innocence.

Rolls Canardly A bomb car.

ronny Sexual intercourse. From rhyming slang **Ronny Coote** for root.

roo 1. A kangaroo. 2. A jackaroo.

roo bar An extra steel bumper bar, or bull bar, on a vehicle that helps protect the vehicle from damage caused by colliding with kangaroos, and other animals, on the road.

a **rooster one day and a feather duster the next** A phrase indicating the ups and downs of life.

root 1. To have sexual intercourse. 2. An act of sexual intercourse. 3. To kick.

rootable Sexually desirable.

root a dog on a chain Of a male, to be randy or desperate for sex.

rooted 1. Exhausted, e.g. 'I'm really rooted after that run'. 2. Something that is broken or wrecked.

rooter or **root rat**. Someone noted for their rooting.

root ute A panel van fitted out in the back with a mattress and curtains as a venue for sexual liaisons. Also **fuck truck**.

root your boot Another way of saying get lost or get knicked.

ropeable Very angry or seething.

rort 1. A deceptive scheme or lurk. Also a job that is a bit easy, and dodgy practices indulged in by politicians. 2. A wild party.

rorter Someone who perpetrates a rort.

Rose Bay shopping trolley Sydney slang for a city-only four-wheel-drive.

rotgut Cheap, nasty liquor.

rotten Very drunk.

rough Unfair or unjust, e.g. 'I think you were a bit rough on her'.

rough as bags Extremely rough or uncouth. Also **rough as guts** and **rough as hessian undies**.

rough diamond A fair dinkum, honest person without refinement.

rough end of the pineapple To get the worst end or a raw deal.

roughie 1. A starter that runs at long odds and therefore has little chance of winning. 2. A rough or crude person. 3. A swindle.

rough it To live without the comforts of home.

rough trot A run of bad luck.

rouseabout Someone employed to do odd jobs on a rural property. Also **roustabout**.

rouse on or **rouse at** To scold someone.

royal flush A prank in which someone's head is shoved into a toilet which is then flushed.

Royce A fart. From rhyming slang Royce Hart.

RS Another way of saying **rat shit**.

rub-a-dub-dub Rhyming slang for pub.

rubber 1. Car tyres. To **burn rubber** or **lay down rubber** is to drive aggressively. 2. A condom.

rubber neck A stickybeak. Also a derogatory term for a tourist. To idly gaze at things is **rubbernecking**.

rubber nut An annoying person.

rubbish To put down someone.

rubbity Shortened version of **rubbity dub**, rhyming slang for pub.

rub uglies To have sex.

ruckus A commotion.

ruddy Euphemism for bloody.

rude bits The genitalia.

rug up To dress warmly, e.g. 'It's bloody freezing out there, you'd better rug up'.

rule The best or the greatest, e.g. 'Aussies rule'.

Rules Australian Rules Football.

rum Odd or strange.

rum do A lively party. A common term in Tasmania.

run a banker A full river or creek.

runaround If someone is **giving you the runaround** they are being evasive or fobbing you off.

run-in A dispute or a quarrel.

run like a dog To run slowly or poorly.

run of outs A succession of bad luck.

run-through Of a male, an act of sexual intercourse.

rush A feeling of exhilaration as in a **rush of blood**.

Ruski Derogatory term for a Russian.

rust bucket A vehicle that is riddled with rust.

S

sack 1. When you are fired from your job, you **get the sack**. 2. Bed. To **hit the sack** is to go to bed.

sack of shit A lazy, good-for-nothing person.

sacred site A place of great significance for the individual. This is a jocular extension of the concept of the Aboriginal sacred site.

saddling paddock A place where sexual activities take place.

safe as a bank Something that is very safe or certain.

said the actress to the bishop A phrase used to make a sexual innuendo out of an innocent statement.

salad dodger An obese person.

Sallie Abbreviation for a member of the Salvation Army. Also **Sal** or **Salvo**. **The Sallies** or **the Salvos** is the Salvation Army.

salmon A $20 note, so called because of its colour.

saltie A saltwater crocodile.

salt mine The workplace.

salute The Aussie practice of brushing away flies from the face. Also called the **Aussie salute**.

salute the judge To win a race, particularly a horse race.

sambo A sandwich. Also **sammo**.

same diff No difference.

same ol', same ol' The usual thing.

Sandgroper Someone who lives in the state of WA.

sandshoe crusher In cricket, a ball aimed at the feet of the batsman.

Sandy McNab Rhyming slang for cab.

sanger or **sanga** 1. A sandwich. 2. A sausage.

sanno The man who was employed to empty sanitary cans before flush toilets.

Santa Claus The fluffy airborne seed of various plants. Also a **Father Christmas**, **fairy**, **robber** or a **wish**.

sarky Abbreviation of sarcastic.

sarvo This afternoon, e.g. 'I'll be round there sarvo'.

satched Soaked through. Short for saturated.

satchel swinger A bookmaker.

sausage 1. The penis. 2. **Not a sausage** is absolutely nothing.

sausage roll Rhyming slang for an Aussie Rules goal.

saver To have a secondary bet on another competitor to offset money already wagered.

sawbones A surgeon.

sawn-off A short person.

SBD Inaudible flatulence that is very smelly. Stands for 'Silent But Deadly'.

scab 1. A mean or stingy person. 2. A person who cadges from others. 3. To cadge or borrow without intending to pay back. 4. Someone who breaks a strike by working. 5. Someone who sorts through rubbish to find something they think is valuable.

scabby 1. Poor quality or bad. 2. Someone who is mean or contemptible.

scag Heroin.

scale To board public transport without paying the fare.

scaly The operator of a weighbridge.

scallywag A rascal or mischievous person.

scarce as rocking horse shit Something that is very scarce. Also **scarce as hen's teeth**.

Schindler's Drunk. Short for Schindler's List, rhyming slang for pissed.

schizo A schizophrenic or someone who is crazy.

schlock Low-grade entertainment.

schmick 1. Cool or excellent, e.g. 'That's a really schmick car'. Also **smick** or **schmicko**. 2. Neat and tidy. 3. To get **schmicked up** is to get dressed up.

schmo A foolish person.

schmooze 1. Idle chat. 2. To try to impress an important person.

schnozz The nose. Also **schnozza** and **schnozzle**.

schooie Short term for a schooner of beer.

school 1. A group of people taking turns at buying the drinks at the pub. 2. A gathering of gamblers.

schoolie 1. A school student. 2. A holidaying student who has just completed their final school exams. 3. A school prawn.

schoolies week A week's holiday taken by school students after their final-year exams.

schooner A beer glass of 15 fluid ounces in all states except SA where it is a 10 fluid ounce glass.

schtick A stage routine or a gimmick.

schwing A cool way of saying swing in reference to music and dancing.

scoff To eat in a hurry or to gobble down.

scone 1. Your head. 2. To strike on the head. Also **sconed**.

scoob A marijuana joint.

scope To look about.

scorcher A very hot day.

score 1. The latest news, e.g. 'What's the score on that development?' 2. The customer of a prostitute. 3. $20. 4. To get or obtain, e.g. 'I've just scored another job'. 5. To obtain a partner for casual sex. 6. To obtain illegal drugs. 7. To win a race or a contest.

Scott Neville An unpopular bloke who has no friends.

scotty Annoyed or irritable.

scozzer A Victorian term for a bogan or a westie.

scrag 1. An unkempt person. 2. A derogatory term for a woman. 3. A blokey word for sexual intercourse.

scranno A coffee break or a smoko.

scrap 1. A fight or a dispute, e.g. 'There was a bit of a scrap at the pub'. 2. A bicycle.

scrape 1. An act of sexual intercourse. 2. An abortion.

scratch Money.

scratchie 1. An instant lottery ticket. 2. In Victoria, a public transport ticket.

screamer 1. Someone who gets drunk very quickly, e.g. 'He's a two-pot screamer'. 2. A spectacular effort, such as a great mark in Aussie Rules. 3. Someone who is very vocal during sexual intercourse.

screw 1. To have sexual intercourse. 2. To ruin or wreck something is to **screw it** or **screw it up**. 3. Used as a term of abuse and in a similar way to 'damn'. 4. A prison warder. 5. To have a look. 6. A wage.

screw about 1. To engage in casual sex or to cheat on someone sexually. 2. To waste time. 3. To treat unfairly. Also **screw around**.

screwed Something that is ruined or wrecked.

screw up 1. To make a mistake. 2. To ruin something.

screw with To meddle with someone or something.

scrote The scrotum.

scrounge To search through rubbish for food or valuables.

scrub Bush country.

scrub basher An old vehicle used for bashing around in the bush.

scrubber 1. An unattractive woman of questionable morals. 2. A cow or bull gone feral. 3. A horse bred in the wild and seen as inferior. 4. A racehorse that is not much good. 5. A grey kangaroo.

scrub up To do yourself up with clothes and grooming, e.g. 'She scrubs up pretty well'.

scrummy Scrumptious or delicious.

scum 1. Contemptible people. 2. To cadge something.

scumbag A contemptible person. Also **scumball** or **scumbucket**.

scum of the earth The worst kind of person, e.g. 'That family, they're the scum of the earth'.

scum on To rebuke someone.

scum sucker A contemptible person.

scunge 1. Someone who takes no pride in his or her personal appearance. 2. Filth or dirt. 3. To cadge. 4. A stingy person.

scunge-face A contemptible person.

scungies Women's full brief underpants worn while playing sport. Also **bum-shorts**, **bummers**, **bloomers** and **runners**.

scungy Mean, unpleasant or of inferior quality.

scunted Caught in the act.

scuzz A contemptible person. Also **scuzzbag**, **scuzzball** and **scuzzbucket**.

sea-changer Someone who has moved to a quieter coastal area after living in a city.

seagull 1. Someone working in a job that requires them to fly in and fly out in a plane or helicopter, such as on an oil rig. 2. A non-union dock worker. 3. Someone who makes a lot of fuss, upsets everyone and then leaves. 4. A visiting tourist.

secko A sex pervert or a sex offender.

see a man about a dog A phrase used when leaving a gathering to go to the toilet.

seedy 1. Gross or dodgy. 2. Describes feeling the effects of a big drinking session. 3. A sexual pervert.

sell someone a pup To swindle or cheat someone.

semi 1. A semi-trailer. 2. A semi-detached house.

send her down Huey A plea to the gods to make it rain.

send up To satirise something or someone, or to mock.

septic tank Rhyming slang for Yank, or an American.

serve Extreme admonishment, e.g. 'He copped a real serve from the boss'.

servo A service station.

session 1. A period of time spent drinking. 2. Time spent smoking dope. 3. An extended bout of lovemaking. 4. A period of surfing.

set 1. A pair of large breasts. 2. A series of large waves. 3. Having a bet placed in racing.

settle petal Relax, don't get uptight. Usually directed to a female but also used for men who may be acting a bit precious.

seven A 7 fluid ounce beer glass.

seven course meal A six pack of beer and a meat pie.

sex, drugs and rock 'n' roll To enjoy a life of partying, drinking, drugs and casual sex.

sex on legs A very sexually attractive person. Also **sex on a stick**.

shack A simple cottage.

shackle dragger A derogatory term for an Australian. It refers to the nation's convict origins.

shack up To live together in a sexual relationship.

shades Sunglasses.

shagged To be exhausted after a long session of sexual intercourse.

shagger A person noted for their sexual activities.

shagger's back Back complaint usually attributed to too much sex.

shaggin' wagon A panel van that could be used for sexual pleasures.

shake To steal.

shake hands with the unemployed Of a male, to urinate. Also **shake hands with the wife's best friend**.

shake the cow To shake a milk carton to see how much milk is left in it.

shake the hairy lettuce Of a woman, to urinate.

shaking like a kangaroo dog crouching over a thistle To be shivering or shaking with cold or fear.

the **Shaky Isles** New Zealand.

shandy A mix of beer and lemonade.

shanghai 1. A catapult. Also slingshot. 2. To compel someone to do something they don't want to do.

shank 1. To make a mistake. 2. To incorrectly hit a golf ball.

Shanks' pony To use your legs as a mode of transport. First recorded in Britain in 1785 as 'shanks-nag' in R. Fergusson's *Poems* where mention is made of the need to walk as the nag was tired. Has been in use in Australia since colonial times.

shark bait Someone who swims where there is danger of a shark attack.

shark biscuit 1. A new surfer. 2. A bodyboard rider. 3. A cheap foam surfboard. 4. A bodyboard.

shark feeding frenzy A mob of people clambering over each other to get to something, for example at a post-Christmas sale.

sharpie A teenage or young adult hoodlum.

shat off To be fed up or disappointed.

she Any object, person or occurrence, e.g. 'She'll be right mate'.

sheep station A supposed prize for a contest or a sporting match, as used in 'We're not playing for sheep stations'.

sheetie A sheet metal worker.

sheik A term used by women to describe a dashing, debonair man.

sheila A woman. Used since the 1830s and is a generic use of the common Irish girl's name.

shekels Money.

shelf An informer or to inform upon. Underworld slang since the 1920s and taken from the phrase 'on the shelf', or out of the way.

shellacking A heavy defeat, e.g. 'They copped a real shellacking'.

she'll be right Everything will be all right.

she looks like she's been pulled through a hollow log backwards Describes an unattractive woman.

she-men Muscular women.

shemozzle A confused state of affairs.

sherbet A beer, e.g. 'I'm just going for a few sherbets'.

she's sweet Everything is fine.

shickered or **shicker** Drunk.

shindig A party.

shiner A black eye.

a **shingle short** Someone lacking full intelligence.

shiny arse Someone who works behind a desk. Also a **shiny bum**.

the **Shire** The common name used for the Sutherland Shire of Sydney.

shirt-front A bruising, head-on tackle in Aussie Rules.

shirt lifter A homosexual male.

shirty To get upset or to be in a bad mood.

shish kebab A euphemism for shit.

shit 1. To defecate. Also excrement. 2. To anger someone. 3. To mislead or deceive. Also **bullshit**. 4. A contemptible person. 5. Junk or rubbish. 6. To talk nonsense or rubbish. 7. A word of abuse. 8. Drugs. 9. Very bad.

shit a brick Damn or hell.

shit-awful Dreadful.

shitbag To denigrate someone.

shit box 1. A dirty house. 2. A hopeless car. 3. A contemptible person.

shit bucket A bucket or can used for a toilet.

shitcan To severely criticise someone or something.

shit catchers Knickerbockers.

shite A euphemism for shit.

shit-easy Something that is terribly easy.

shit end of the stick The worst part of a deal.

shitface A contemptible person.

shit-faced Very drunk.

shit for brains A stupid or brainless person.

shit happens A term of resignation after suffering misfortune. Also **shit happens, then you die** and **shit happens, arseholes cause it**.

shithead A contemptible person.

shit heap A crappy car.

shit hole A filthy, disgusting place.

shit-hot Extremely good.

shithouse 1. A toilet. 2. Something that is terrible or foul.

shit in your own nest To have a relationship with a colleague.

shit it in To win easily or to do something with ease.

shit itself A mechanical gadget that has stopped working or is buggered.

shit kicker An assistant who does menial tasks.

shitless Completely, as in bored shitless.

shit list A list of people you hate.

shit load A great deal.

shit of a thing Describes anything that is annoying.

shit off To annoy.

shit on 1. To denigrate. 2. To be better than.

shit on the liver The cause of bad temper.

the **shits** 1. A bad mood. 2. Diarrhoea.

shit scared Frightened or terrified.

shit shoveller Someone who does hard, manual work.

shit stir To make trouble. A **shit-stirrer** does this.

shitter 1. The toilet. 2. The equivalent of hell, e.g. 'He beat the shitter out of me'.

shit tickets Toilet paper.

shitting bricks To be very scared or nervous.

shitty 1. Annoyed. 2. Of poor quality.

shit upon To be better than.

shit work The jobs that no one else wants to do.

shit yourself To be terrified or scared. Also **shitting your pants**.

shivoo A party.

shocker Something dreadfully bad. Known in rhyming slang as a Barry Crocker, e.g. 'He had a real shocker today'.

shock jock A radio host who sensationalises the news.

shonk A dishonest person or a swindler.

shonky 1. Of dubious character or quality. 2. Counterfeit.

shoofty 1. To look or inspect. 2. Dishonest or sneaky.

shoo-in A certainty to win, e.g. 'The favourite's a shoo-in'.

shook on Infatuated with someone.

shoot a fairy To pass wind or fart. Also **shoot a bunny**.

shoot blanks To ejaculate infertile sperm or to experience orgasm without ejaculation.

shooting gallery A venue where people inject heroin.

shoot through To leave or decamp.

shoot through like a Bondi tram To make a hasty departure.

shoot your bolt To ejaculate. Also **shoot your wad**.

shop till you drop A shopping spree.

short and curlies Pubic hair. If someone **has you by the short and curlies** you are in a no-win situation.

short arm The penis.

short arms and long pockets Of someone, to be miserly with their money.

short of Used to describe someone or something that is 'not all there' as in **a shingle short**, **a button short**, **a few bricks short of a load**, **a few sheep short of a paddock**, **a couple of alps short of a range**, **a few bites short of a bickie**, **a few bangers short of a barbie**, **a couple of lamingtons short of a CWA meeting**, **a few sandwiches short of a picnic** or **a few Tim Tams short of a packet**.

shotgun 1. To drink a can of beer by shaking it up a little, puncturing a small hole near the base and then placing the mouth over the hole and releasing the ring pull. 2. A cry made to claim the front passenger seat of a car and can also be made to 'bags' anything.

shot of 1. To be rid of, e.g. 'I can't wait to be shot of that bloke'. 2. Fed up with.

shotty A shotgun.

shouse Euphemism for the shithouse or toilet.

shout 1. When it's your turn to buy the drinks, it's your turn to shout and you are also **in a shout**. 2. To pay for anything for another person, e.g. 'I'll shout you a pie'.

shove off Go away or nick off.

show 1. A chance or an opportunity. 2. A matter of business. 3. A military engagement.

show bag 1. A sample bag of goodies bought at agricultural shows. 2. Someone full of crap. 3. A show-off.

showie The operator of an amusement ride at an agricultural show.

show pony A fancy show-off.

show you the ropes To show someone how to do something.

shrapnel Small change.

shrewdie Someone of great cunning. Also a **shrewd head**.

shrimp A person of small stature.

shrink A psychiatrist.

shut-eye Sleep, e.g. 'I just have to get some shut-eye'.

sick Excellent or cool.

sickie To have a day off work because you are ill, or when you feign illness because you want to do something other than work.

sicko A disturbed person.

sick puppy A depraved person.

side A superior manner or putting on airs and graces.

silent but deadly Of flatulence, that is not audible but smells bad. Also **SBD** or **silent but violent.**

silent cop A small, circular steel traffic device placed at intersections.

silly as ... Very silly. Used in such phrases as **silly as a pork chop**, **silly as a two-bob watch**, **silly as a bum full of Smarties** and **silly as three wet hens in a row**.

silver bullet A can of Reschs Pilsener beer.

Silver City A nickname for the NSW city of Broken Hill.

silver pillow The bladder of a wine cask.

silvertail A derogatory term for someone from the upper crust of society.

sin bin 1. A panel van or station wagon used for sexual pleasures. 2. An area set aside for penalised players who are sent from the field of play for a period of time.

since Archer won the Cup In a long time. Also **since Adam was a pup**.

Sin City A derisive nickname for Sydney.

the **Singing Budgie** A nickname for singer Kylie Minogue.

single-barrelled shot gun A big expulsion of snot from the nose. Also a **snot rocket**.

sink To drink a glass of alcohol. Usually used as to **sink a few**.

sink the sausage Of a male, to have sexual intercourse.

sink the slipper To kick someone when they are down or to put the boot in.

sixer 1. In cricket, a score of six runs in one hit that clears the boundary. 2. A goal in Aussie rules.

six-finger country A remote area in which the inhabitants are imagined to be inbred.

Six-finger Nationals A derisive term for members of the National Party, many of whom come from remote areas.

six o'clock swill A session of heavy drinking just before 6 p.m. as this was when the pubs closed up until 1955.

sixpack Well-defined abdominal muscles of a man.

six-pointer 1. A converted try in rugby league. 2. Three slices of bread with filling, cut diagonally.

sixty-nine Simultaneous oral sex by two people.

skank 1. An ugly or filthy person, male or female. 2. A promiscuous woman.

skanky Filthy or contemptible.

skatie A skateboard rider.

skating on thin ice To be living dangerously or doing something very risky.

skeeter 1. A mosquito. 2. A man of small build.

skeg A derogatory term for a surfie. Also **skeg head**.

skerrick The tiniest amount.

skid lid A motorcycle crash helmet.

skid mark A mark or smudge made by excrement on underwear. Also **skiddies**.

skimpy A scantily clad barmaid.

skin and blister Rhyming slang for sister.

skin flick A pornographic movie.

skinful To have drunk a lot of alcohol is to have **had a skinful**.

skinner A horse at long odds that wins a race and 'skins' the punters.

skinny Coffee made with skim milk.

skint Broke.

skip hop Australian hip-hop music.

skirt A woman viewed as a sex object.

skite To brag or show off.

skol To consume a drink in one go.

sky rocket Rhyming slang for pocket.

slab 1. A carton of 24 cans or stubbies of beer. 2. $1000. 3. A preparation table at a morgue or mortuary.

slack 1. Very lazy. 2. No good or hopeless. 3. Unkind or mean. 4. Of a woman, promiscuous. Also **slack moll**.

slack arse A lazy person.

slacker Anyone who avoids hard work.

slag 1. To spit. 2. A derogatory term for a promiscuous or contemptible woman.

slag off To denigrate someone.

slammer Jail.

slanter Any form of dishonest trickery.

slant-eye A racist term for any Asian person.

slap bang Exactly right.

slap dash To do a quick and rough job.

slapping skins Having sexual intercourse.

slash 1. Of a male, to urinate. 2. The vagina.

slaughtered Very drunk.

sleaze A contemptible man who mistakenly thinks all women find him attractive. Also occasionally applied to women who are overtly sexual in an unpleasant manner.

sleazebag A sleazy person or a contemptible person. Also **scumbag**, **sleazeball**, **sleazoid** or **sleazebucket**.

sleazepit A nightclub or bar full of sleazy people.

sledging Heaping abuse or ridicule on members of the opposing team in a sporting contest.

sleepout A partially enclosed verandah used as sleeping quarters.

sleep over Of children, to sleep for a night at the house of a friend.

slew 1. A large number. 2. To turn your head or look sideways. 3. To defeat.

slime 1. A sleazy person. To slime onto someone is to try to seduce them in a sleazy way. 2. A contemptible person. Also **slimebag**, **slimeball** or **slimebucket**.

sling 1. To give money as a bribe. 2. A gratuity or tip.

sling off To disparage someone.

slingshot A child's catapult. Also a **dinger**, a **ging**, a **gonk** or a **shanghai**.

sling your hook To depart.

slip The price of a fare home given to a punter who has lost all their money.

slipper When someone is kicked they have copped the slipper and have become a **sink the slipper** victim.

slip someone a length Of a man, to have sexual intercourse.

slog Hard work.

slop Choppy sea.

slope A racist term for an Asian. Also **slopehead**.

slops Beer. To have a drinking session is to be **on the slops**.

slops merchant A lover of beer.

sloshed Very drunk.

slot A prison cell.

slouch hat The iconic hat of an Aussie soldier.

slug 1. A lazy person. 2. The penis.

sluggos Speedos or men's swimming briefs. Also **sluggies**, **sluggers** or **slug-huggers**. Among the many other names are **ball huggers**, **boasters**, **budgie smugglers**, **cluster busters**, **cock chokers**, **cock jocks** (or **CJs**), **cod jocks**, **dick bathers**,

dick pointers, **dick pokers** (or **DPs**), **dick stickers**, **dick togs** (or **DTs**), **dipsticks**, **fish frighteners**, **knobbies**, **lolly bags**, **meat hangers**, **racers**, **scungies** and **toolies.**

slug it out To fight.

slurry Derogatory for a promiscuous woman or a slut.

slush box Derogatory name for a car with automatic transmission.

slushy A cook's assistant or kitchen hand.

sly grog Illegally made or supplied alcohol. A person who supplies it is a **sly grogger** and the place it is obtained is a **sly groggery**.

smack Heroin.

smacked out Under the influence of heroin.

smacker A dollar. Also a **smackeroo** or a **smackeroonie**.

smackhead Someone addicted to heroin. Also a **smackie**.

smart alec A know-it-all.

smart arse A person who likes showing off.

smarty pants A show-off or know-it-all.

smashed Drunk or stoned on drugs.

smasher Someone who is very attractive to the opposite sex.

smell Someone who won't leave you alone is said to be **hanging around like a bad smell**.

smiling like a mother-in-law in a divorce court To be very happy.

smoko A break from work to have a cigarette, or now more likely to be for a coffee. Also **smoke-oh** or **smoke-o**.

smokie A horse whose form has been kept secret.

smooch To kiss and cuddle.

smooey The female genitalia. A **bit of smooey** is sex with a woman. Also **smoo**.

smoush or **smoosh** A long kiss.

smut 1. To kiss passionately. 2. Depraved sexual material.

snafu A chaotic situation. Stands for 'Situation normal: All fucked up'.

snag 1. A sausage. 2. A problem.

SNAG A new-age type male who is sensitive and articulate. It stands for 'Sensitive New-Age Guy'.

snagger A poor or bad shearer.

snail mail The normal postal service as opposed to e-mail.

snail trail Dried mucus or semen on clothing.

snake bite A drink of Guinness and apple cider.

Snake Gully A mythical remote place.

snake oil merchant Someone who sells phoney medical treatments.

snake's hiss Rhyming slang for piss.

snaky Annoyed or touchy.

snapping log A crocodile.

snark A male who sniffs girl's bicycle seats.

snatch The female genitalia.

snatch it To quit a job.

snig To pull or drag timber logs.

snodger Excellent or awesome.

snoozer 1. Any bloke. 2. A senior citizen.

snork 1. A sausage. 2. A baby or young child.

snorkel The penis.

snot block 1. A vanilla slice. This term is mainly used in Victoria. Also a **snot box** or a **snot brick**. 2. A small plastic box filled with gel used to protect joints of electrical wiring. Also a **snotty**.

snot rag A handkerchief.

snot rocket An explosion of snot from the nose.

snot someone To hit or bash someone.

snow Cocaine.

snow bird Someone travelling with a caravan. Believed to originate from the traits of many birds who fly north or south to escape the cold weather.

snowdrop To steal laundry from a clothes line.

snoz The nose. Short for **schnozzle**.

snuff it To die.

soak A heavy alcohol drinker.

soapy Smelly and dirty. Someone who doesn't like washing.

sobriety challenged Drunk.

so bucktoothed he/she could eat a watermelon through a barbed wire fence Describes someone with buck teeth or protruding top teeth.

sod A contemptible person. Can also be used affectionately, e.g. 'He's a poor old sod'.

soda Something that is easy to do.

soft cock An ineffectual or weak person.

soft cock rock Weak and wimpy rock music.

soft touch A generous person who readily lends money or does favours.

soldier A strip of toast for dipping into a soft-boiled egg.

solid Thoroughly or completely.

sook A sensitive or soft person.

sooky Timid or cowardly.

sool Inciting a dog to attack, e.g. 'If you don't leave, I'll sool the dog onto you'.

sop 1. A weak person. 2. Stale white bread and dripping soaked in hot water and eaten with tomato sauce and salt. Also **Pop's sop**.

sort A good-looking female.

sorted Dealt with or fixed up, e.g. 'Don't worry mate, the car's sorted'.

so unlucky he'd be killed by a tsunami in the Simpson Desert To be extremely unlucky.

southerly buster A strong, cool southerly wind that blows after a hot day on the south-eastern coast of Australia.

South Seas Pom Derogatory term for a New Zealander. Also **South Pacific Pom**.

souvenir To steal a minor item in order to keep as a souvenir.

sozzled Drunk.

spac A general insult used by young people and meaning uncool, stupid or clumsy. Also **spacca** and **spacko**.

space cadet A vague or stupid person.

spaced out In a dreamy state and usually brought about by drugs although it can also be caused by tiredness or illness.

spacey 1. Vague or empty-headed. 2. Hallucinatory.

spacies Computer arcade games. Named after one such game, Space Invaders.

spade 1. An attempt to impress a potential sexual partner. Short for **spade work**. 2. A racist term for a person with dark skin.

spag 1. Short for spaghetti. 2. Derogatory term for an Italian. 3. A sparrow. 4. Saliva or mucus that is spat out.

spag bol Spaghetti bolognaise. Also **spag bog**.

Spanish dancer Rhyming slang for cancer.

spanner head A car enthusiast.

spare tyre A roll of fat around someone's midriff.

sparrow fart Dawn, e.g. 'He gets up at sparrow fart to go to work'.

spastic 1. A foolish or clumsy person. 2. To **go spastic** is to have a tantrum. Also **chuck a spastic**. 3. Very drunk.

spaz A shortening of spastic. Also **spazzo**. To **chuck a spaz** is to lose your cool. A **spaz attack** An instance of losing your cool.

spear To get the spear is to be given the sack or be retrenched from work.

spear the bearded clam Of a male, to have sexual intercourse.

speccy 1. Spectacular or impressive. 2. A great mark in Aussie Rules.

speck 1. To search the ground for precious stones or metals. 2. To bet in a speculative manner at the races.

speedball A rissole.

speed merchant Someone who likes driving fast. Also **speed demon**.

Speed Gordon To be **in more trouble than Speed Gordon** is to be in a lot of trouble. This was the name under which American comic book hero Flash Gordon was known in Australia for some time.

speed hump A derisive term used by boat enthusiasts for a skindiver.

spew 1. To vomit or the vomit itself. 2. To be upset or disappointed with someone. Also **spewing**.

spewsome Nauseating.

spewy 1. Unpleasant. 2. To be in a bad mood.

spiel A speech designed to explain and sell a product.

spieler A con artist who uses speech to deceive others.

spike the keg To urinate for the first time during a drinking session. Also **break the seal**.

spill the beans To divulge information. In many cases this information should not be shared. Also **spill your guts**.

spin a yarn To tell a tall story. Also **spin a dit**.

spinebashing Being in bed sleeping, resting or ill.

spinifex grasshopper A kangaroo.

spinner The person tossing the coins up in a game of two-up.

spin out 1. Causing amazement or shock. 2. In two-up, to lose the right to spin the coins by throwing a pair of tails.

spit 1. To vomit. 2. To be angry. Also **spit the dummy** or **spit chips**.

spit it out A plea to say what you have to say.

spit the dummy To throw a temper tantrum. It refers to a baby throwing a tantrum and spitting out its dummy.

spiv A flashy man who lives by his wits, without working and often by dubious activity.

splash the boots To urinate.

split the whiskers Of a woman, to urinate.

splosh Money.

spondonicles Metal tongs used to lift the hot billy off the fire. Also **spongs** or **billy grips**.

spondulicks Money. Also **spondula, spondulee, spons** or **spon**. Originally British slang from the 1850s and believed to be derived from the ancient Greek word *spondulikos* for a round stone or weight, a voting pebble.

sponger Someone who lives off the efforts of others. Also a **bludger**.

spoof Semen.

spoon A fool.

sport 1. An affectionate nickname for a fellow or bloke. 2. A fair-minded person. Also a **good sport**.

spot on Exactly right.

spottie A spotlight.

spotto A game played on long road trips in which the first person to see a designated object calls out 'spotto'.

the **Spout** A derisive nickname in Canberra for the Captain Cook Fountain.

spray-on trousers Very tight-fitting trousers.

spray the bowl This is what happens when you are suffering from diarrhoea.

spring 1. To be caught in the act of doing something wrong. Also **sprung**. 2. To help someone escape from jail.

springy A wetsuit covering the body to the elbows, knees and neck.

sprog 1. A child. 2. A new recruit. 3. Semen.

spruik To make a speech and particularly to sell a product or attract an audience. A **spruiker** is someone who spruiks to attract customers to a show.

spud 1. A potato. A **spud cocky** is a potato farmer, and a region where potatoes are grown is **spud country**. 2. A hole in a sock with the skin showing through. 3. A fist, and thus **spuds** is another name for the game rock, paper scissors.

spunk 1. A good-looking, sexy member of the opposite sex. 2. Semen.

spunkette An attractive and sexy female.

spunky Someone who is good looking and sexy. Also **spunkalicious**, **spunk bubble** or **spunk rat**.

square 1. A daggy person or one who is ignorant of popular culture. 2. A heterosexual person. 3. A law-abiding person.

square bear A 750ml bottle of Bundaberg Rum.

squashed fly biscuit A biscuit with dried fruit between two thin layers of pastry. Also **dead fly biscuit** or a **fly cemetery**.

squat Nothing or none. Short for **diddly-squat**.

squatter 1. In colonial times, someone who settled on crown land to run stock initially without permission but later with a lease. 2. One of a group of rich and influential landholders. Also **squattocracy**.

squeal To inform on someone or to reveal something secret.

squealie Making the tyres of a car squeal.

squib 1. Someone who shirks an issue or situation and usually in a cowardly manner. To **squib it** is to act in a cowardly way. 2. A racehorse or greyhound that starts well but finishes badly. Also **damp squib**.

squillion An extremely large amount. Also a **squintillion**. Someone with a squillion is a **squillionaire** or a **squintillionaire**.

squirrel grip To grab and squeeze someone's testicles.

squirt 1. A small or insignificant person. 2. A child. 3. Male urination.

squitters Diarrhoea.

squiz To take a look at something or someone.

stack An accident or a fall.

stacked A woman with large breasts.

stack on To put something on. To **stack on a blue** is to become very angry. To **stack on an act** or **stack on a turn** is to make a big fuss over nothing.

stacks Many or plenty, e.g. 'Come over, I've got stacks of beer'.

stack up zeds To sleep.

staffies After work drinks for the staff.

stag film A pornographic film.

stairway to heaven A ladder in a woman's stocking.

stalk An erect penis.

stallion A sexually active man.

stand out like dog's balls To be conspicuous.

stand over To intimidate someone.

standover merchant Someone who bullies or intimidates.

starkers 1. Totally naked. 2. Insane or stark raving mad.

Starlight Hotel Sleeping under the stars.

starver A saveloy.

starve the lizards An exclamation of surprise or amazement. Also **stiffen the lizards** or **stone the crows**.

stash A cache of drugs for personal use.

statie A state or public school student.

Steak and Kidney Rhyming slang for Sydney.

steamer A lightweight one-piece wetsuit.

stemmy A schoolboy term for the penis.

St Georges Terrace cocky In WA, a person who lives in the city and who owns a country property, often for tax avoidance purposes.

stick 1. An affectionate term for an old person, e.g. 'She's not a bad old stick'. 2. A very thin person. 3. A surfboard. 4. The penis. **Up the stick** means pregnant and **had the stick** means ruined or wrecked. 5. An injection of a drug.

stick book A pornographic magazine. Also **stick mag**.

sticker licker In SA, a parking inspector.

stickjaw A very sticky toffee.

stick like shit to a blanket To adhere very well or to cling to.

the **sticks** 1. A location well outside the city and usually in the bush or the outback. 2. The goal posts in Aussie Rules.

stick sister A woman who knowingly shares a man with another woman.

stickybeak 1. An inquisitive or nosy person. 2. A look to satisfy your own inquisitive nature. 3. A black seed that sticks to clothing.

stiff 1. A dead body. 2. Unlucky. 3. An erect penis. Also **stiffy**. 4. A letter sent in or out of prison illicitly.

stiff cheese Bad luck or sucked in. Also **stiff cheddar**, **stiff luck** or **stiff shit** and often shortened to **stiff**.

stiffener An alcoholic drink.

stiffen the crows An exclamation of surprise or amazement. Also **stone the crows**, **stiffen the lizards** and **stiffen the wombats**.

stiffo Tough luck.

sting 1. A con trick or scam. 2. A police undercover operation. 3. A drug given to a racehorse to make it run faster. 4. A strong drink.

stink bomb The seed of some acacia species which give off a foul smell.

stinker 1. A hot and humid day. 2. An unpleasant person or thing. 3. A black eye. 4. A western grey kangaroo.

stinko Drunk.

stipe A stipendiary steward at a racecourse.

stir 1. To taunt or tease. 2. Prison.

stir-crazy Crazy due to being in prison.

stirrer Someone who is always causing trouble.

stir the possum To create a disturbance.

stoked To be very pleased or amazed.

stoned 1. Under the influence of drugs. 2. Very drunk.

stone motherless last To come last.

stone the crows The most commonly used exclamation of surprise or amazement. Also **stiffen the crows** and **starve the lizards**.

stonker 1. To stop someone in their tracks or to defeat in a competition. 2. To make very drunk.

stonkered 1. Totally drunk. 2. Satisfied after a large meal. 3. Defeated or outdone.

store jack A security officer in a store.

storm and strife Rhyming slang for wife.

stoush 1. A fight or argument. World War I is also known as **the Big Stoush**. 2. To fight with someone.

straightie A conservative, or straight, person. Also a **straightie 180**.

strain the potatoes or **strain the spuds**. Of a male, to urinate.

strawb Shortening of strawberry.

street cred Status among people of the trendy, fashionable set.

streetie 1. A street kid. 2. A street prostitute.

stress head A person who is easily stressed.

stretch 1. A term of imprisonment, e.g. 'He was in for a two-year stretch'. 2. A form of address to a tall person.

stretcher case A sportsperson who is carried from the field unconscious. Also anyone who needs to be carried on a stretcher.

strewth or **struth** A great Aussie expression of amazement or shock.

strides Trousers.

strike a light An exclamation of surprise. Also **strike me blue**, **strike me dead**, **strike me fat**, **strike me handsome**, **strike me pink**, **strike me lucky**, **strike me** or just **strike**.

Strine The broad Australian dialect and pronunciation, e.g. Emma Chisit for 'how much is it?'

stroke mag A pornographic magazine.

stroppy To be in a bad mood or to be difficult.

strut your stuff To proudly display your skills.

Stuart Diver Rhyming slang for survivor. Named after the sole survivor of the Thredbo landslide disaster in 1997.

stubby A 375ml beer bottle, or a beer bottle of similar size.

stubby holder A holder for a stubby or beer can which keeps the cold beer insulated from the heat. Also **stubby cooler**.

stubbies Workers' shorts.

stuck-up Vain or conceited.

stud magnet A woman found attractive and sexy by many men.

stud muffin A physically attractive man.

stuff 1. Euphemism for 'fuck' and hence to ruin or wreck. Also **stuff it** and **not give a stuff**. 2. Drugs.

stuff about or **stuff around** To mess around.

stuff-all Nothing.

stuffed 1. To be very tired or exhausted. 2. Full of food.

stuff-up A failure, mistake or 'screw-up'.

stumps To **pull up stumps** is to stop work or stop what you are doing.

stunned like a thousand startled gazelles To be surprised or shocked.

stuvac In NSW a vacation from school, college or university in the lead-up to exams. A shortened form of 'student vacation'. Also **swot vac**.

subbie 1. A subcontractor. 2. A dull or stupid person.

submarine races A non-existent event used as an excuse to go somewhere quiet.

Such is life! An exclamation of resignation to the harsh facts of life and reputed to be the final words of bushranger Ned Kelly before being hanged.

suck 1. To be dreadful, e.g. 'Homework sucks'. Also **sux**. 2. Oral sex.

sucked in Deceived or tricked, and used in the sense that it serves you right. Also **sucko**, **suck eggs**, **suck a rat**, **suck shit**, **suck my arse**, **suck on that** and **suck it harder**.

sucker Someone who is easily deceived.

sucky 1. Crawling. 2. No good or crap. 3. A strong backwash at the base of a wave.

suds Beer. A **suds artist** is a beer drinker.

suffer A gleeful response to another's misfortune.

suffer a recovery Enduring a hangover after a night on the booze.

sugar and spice Rhyming slang for nice.

suicidal 1. Dangerous and gutsy, e.g. 'Taking that wave was a suicidal move'. 2. Excellent.

suicide blonde A woman who has dyed her own hair blonde rather than having it done professionally.

suit A derogatory term for a businessman or woman.

sunbeam A plate or utensil laid out but not used at a meal.

sundowner A swagman who arrives at a homestead at nightfall and too late for work.

sunnies Sunglasses.

Sunshine stilettos Melbourne slang for daggy suede moccasins and named after the suburb of Sunshine.

super Full-strength beer as opposed to **unleaded**.

sure as shit Without a doubt.

sure beats shovelling shit A job or task that is bad, but not that bad.

sure thing 1. A certainty. 2. A racehorse or greyhound tipped to win. 3. A woman who is a definite chance for sex.

surfboard Women's slang for a large sanitary napkin.

surfie A surfing devotee. Also **surfer**.

surfie chick A female who hangs around surfies and is part of the surfing subculture.

suss 1. Something or someone that is suspicious. 2. Unreliable. 3. To figure out, e.g. 'I sussed that situation out just in time'.

suss it out To check something out.

swag 1. Rolled up bedding and belongings as carried by a swagman. 2. A covered bedroll made from canvas. 3. An unspecified but large number.

swagman A drifter, tramp or hobo who carried his possessions in a swag. Also a **swaggie**.

swamp donkey An imbecile.

swamp hog Derisive term for an unattractive woman.

swampy A surfer.

swanger The penis.

swap spit To French kiss.

swear like a trooper To swear strongly and often.

sweet All right or okay, e.g. 'Don't worry, everything's sweet'.

sweet cop An easy job or task.

Sweet Fanny Adams A polite way of saying 'sweet fuck all' or nothing. Also **SFA** or **sweet FA**.

swiftie A con job or swindle.

swing the bag To work as a bookmaker.

swing the lead To be idle or lazy when there is work to be done.

swipe To take or steal something.

switch hitter A bisexual.

swot vac A vacation from school, college or university in the lead-up to exams to allow students to study. Also **stuvac**.

swy Another name for the game of two-up.

Sydney Harbour Rhyming slang for barber.

Sydney or the bush All or nothing.

sypho Slang version of syphilis.

syphon the python Of a male, to urinate.

T

ta Thank you.

ta ta Goodbye. If you are **going ta tas** you are going away or on a trip.

tacker A young child.

tack-o-rama Completely tacky.

tad A little bit, e.g. 'She was a tad shy'.

taddie A tadpole.

tadpoling Catching tadpoles in the wild.

tag 1. A name for the schoolyard game of chasey. 2. To follow an opponent closely in Aussie Rules, or a **tagger**. 3. The signature of a graffiti artist, or a **tagger**.

tag dag Someone with the shirt tag sticking out of their collar.

tail 1. The backside. 2. A dismissive term for a woman considered to be a sex object. 3. A person who follows another.

tailor made A pre-made cigarette as opposed to a roll-your-own.

take away the toys but leave the playground To have a hysterectomy.

take down To defraud or cheat someone.

take-down A swindle.

take out To win something.

take the knock To admit that you are unable to settle your debts.

take the micky out of To tease someone or make them look foolish.

take your picture To see a flash of a woman's underpants up her skirt.

talk out of your arse To talk nonsense or crap.

talk the leg off an iron pot Said of someone who talks incessantly.

talk underwater People who won't keep quiet are said to be able to do this. If they never shut up they can **talk 10 feet underwater with a snorkel in their mouth**.

tallie In Queensland a 750ml bottle of beer. Also a **longneck** or **king brown**.

tall poppies A successful person or someone with great status. The Australian penchant for bringing successful people down to size is the **tall poppy syndrome**.

tall timber Very tall people.

tanked Drunk.

tanks Muscular men.

tantie A temper tantrum.

tan track The rectum.

tap dancer Rhyming slang for cancer.

tappet head A car enthusiast. Also a **tappet**.

Tarjey A Target department store pronounced with a French-style accent to make it sound as if it is a haute couture fashion house.

tart 1. A promiscuous woman. 2. A prostitute. 3. Also used for any woman but this use is now rather obsolete. Also a **bonzer tart.**

tart up To adorn or make attractive with cheap ornaments, clothes or cosmetics.

Tasmaniac A Tasmanian resident.

Tassie Abbreviation of Tasmania.

taw 1. A playing marble. 2. A hopscotch marker.

tax To steal, e.g. 'That girl taxed my pencil'.

taxi! A call used to indicate that someone is drunk and probably should go home.

tea The evening meal and usually the main meal of the day.

tea leaf Rhyming slang for thief.

tear-arse To travel rapidly.

teasy Irritable.

tea-towel head A racist term for someone from the Middle East. Also **towel head**.

technicolour yawn To vomit.

teddy bear Rhyming slang for lair.

tee up To organise something, e.g. 'Have you teed up that job for tomorrow?'

telly The television.

temporary Australian Someone who rides a motorcycle without wearing proper protective gear.

ten A 10 fluid ounce beer glass. Also a **middy** or **pot**.

Tennant Creek Rhyming slang for Greek.

tenner A $10 note.

Territory confetti The ring pulls from beer cans. So called because it is very warm in the Northern Territory meaning that the locals tend to drink more beer and litter the ground with ring pulls.

terrorist A derisive term for a tourist as viewed by the locals.

Terry toon A pimp. From the rhyming slang for hoon.

thank your mother for the rabbits An old way of saying farewell.

thatch 1. The hair covering the head. 2. Pubic hair.

that's the shot The right way to go about something.

that's the way the cookie crumbles Such is life, that's the way it goes.

the best thing since sliced bread Something that is very good or excellent.

them's fighting words Disagreement or mild anger.

them's the breaks Such is life, there's nothing you can do about it.

the sticks The country, e.g. 'He lives out in the sticks'.

they're all over him like a cheap suit A man who is very popular with women or with everyone.

thick or **thickhead** Someone who is dumb or stupid. Also used in the phrases as **thick as two short planks** or as **thick as a brick**.

thick ear A beating or to hit someone.

thingo Any item or object. Often used if you don't know the name of something, can't think of its name or can't describe it properly. Also **thingy**, **thingummyjig and thingummybob**.

things are crook in Tallarook A situation that is not good. As Tallarook is in Victoria, in NSW it is often substituted with **Muswellbrook** or **Coolongolook**.

think the sun shines out of your arse To have a high opinion of oneself. Also **think your shit doesn't stink**.

third leg The penis.

this arvo This afternoon.

this side of the dirt To be still alive.

thongs Cheap rubber backless sandals.

threads Clothes.

three-dog night A very cold night when you would need three dogs to keep you warm.

threepenny bits Rhyming slang for the shits.

throne The toilet.

throttling pit The toilet.

through to the keeper To allow an insult or a comment to pass without comeback.

throw a Reggie To have a temper tantrum.

throwdown 1. A small firework that explodes when thrown onto the ground. 2. A small bottle of beer.

throw in your marbles To die.

thugby A derogatory term used by AFL fans for rugby union or rugby league. Also used by league fans to describe rugby union.

thunderbags Underpants.

thunderbox The toilet.

thunder thighs Someone with large, fat legs.

tick 1. A short moment in time, e.g. 'Just hang on a tick'. 2. Credit or trust, e.g. 'We bought the vegies on tick'.

ticker 1. The heart. 2. A watch. 3. Bravery or guts, e.g. 'Have you got the ticker to play?'

tickets To have **tickets on yourself** is to have a high opinion of yourself.

tickle the ivories To play the piano.

tickle the peter To rob the cash register.

tick off A stern rebuke or scolding.

tick up To obtain something on credit.

tiddly A little intoxicated.

tiff An argument or dispute, e.g. 'We had a big tiff'.

tiggy tiggy touchwood An Aussie Rules game in which free kicks are continually awarded for minor infringements.

tight 1. Stingy. Also **tight as a bull's arse in fly-time**, **tight as a fish's arsehole** and **tight as a mouse's ear**. 2. Drunk. 3. Close friends.

tight-arse Someone who doesn't like spending their money.

tightwad A stingy person.

a **Tim Tam short of a picnic** Someone who doesn't have full intelligence or is stupid.

Tim Tam suck A treat in which two diagonally opposite corners of a Tim Tam biscuit are bitten off and hot tea or coffee is then sucked through the biscuit. Also **Tim Tam slam** or a **Tim Tam straw**.

tin Money or dosh.

tin arse A lucky person.

tingle A telephone call, e.g. 'Why don't you give her a tingle?'

tin hares Greyhound racing.

tinkle To urinate.

tin lid Rhyming slang for kid.

tinned dog Canned meat.

tinnie 1. Beer in a can. 2. A small aluminium boat.

tinny To be lucky, e.g. 'I was really tinny at the casino yesterday'.

tin tank Rhyming slang for the bank.

tin teeth Orthodontic braces worn on the teeth.

tip A NSW name for the schoolyard game chaseys.

tip-and-run A name for the cricket game in which you have to run every time you hit the ball. Also **tippy-go**, **tippy-go-run**, **tipsy**, **tipsy run** and **hit-and-run**.

tip slinger Someone who gives tips to many different punters in the hope of getting a financial reward if a horse wins.

tip the bucket on someone To denigrate someone.

tit A breast. Also **titty**. If a baby is **on the tit** it is breastfeeding. If **something gets on your tits** it annoys you.

titfer Abbreviation of tit-for-tat, rhyming slang for hat.

titless 1. Without breasts and commonly used disparagingly of flat-chested women. 2. To **scare someone titless** is to frighten them badly.

tits and bums Low-grade entertainment featuring exposed female flesh.

titty hard-ons Erect nipples, especially when showing through clothing.

tizz up To dress up glamorously.

tizzy Hysterical confusion and anxiety. Also a **tizz**.

to-and-from Rhyming slang for Pom.

toastie A toasted sandwich.

tockley The penis.

todge Nonsense or rubbish.

todger The penis.

toecutter A ruthless person.

toe jam Dirt under the toe nails or between the toes.

toe rag A contemptible person.

toey 1. Nervous or edgy, e.g. 'She seems a little toey today'. If you are really toey you are as **toey as a Roman sandal**. 2. Fast or speedy.

togged up Dressed up.

togs 1. Swimmers or a swimsuit. 2. Clothes.

Tojo A Toyota Landcruiser four-wheel-drive.

tomato A red cricket ball.

tombstone A wheelie bin.

tomfoolery 1. Rhyming slang for jewellery. 2. To muck around.

Tom Thumb Rhyming slang for rum.

tomtits Rhyming slang for the shits.

ton 1. 100 miles an hour. 2. A century in cricket. 3. Any score of 100.

tonguey or **tongue-pash** To French kiss.

tonguing Desperate for a drink.

tonk 1. A powerful slog in cricket. 2. A homosexual man. From rhyming slang tonka bean for queen. 3. The penis.

Tonka tough Very tough. From the Tonka brand of heavy-duty toys.

tonsil hockey French kissing.

too cool for school Sophisticated, smart and cooler than cool.

tool 1. An idiot or jerk. 2. The penis.

tool around 1. To fool around. 2. Of a man, to have casual sex with many partners.

toolies Speedos.

tool squeezer A woman seen as a sex object.

too much information Used to rebuke someone for saying something unsavoury or unnecessary.

Toorak tractor Melbourne slang for a city-only four-wheel-drive. Also a **Toorak taxi**.

too right An expression affirming the truth of a statement.

tooshie Angry or upset.

toot A toilet or dunny.

tootsy 1. A foot or toe. 2. Belittling term for a woman.

top The best or excellent. Also **tops**, e.g. 'The party was tops'.

the **Top** The northern part of Australia.

top brass High ranking officers.

Top End The northern part of the Northern Territory.

top-heavy Of a woman, having large breasts.

top notcher A first-rate person.

top off To inform on someone. As a noun a **top-off** is a police informer.

top of the wozza 1. To be in the prime position. 2. Terrific or the best.

torpedo In Aussie Rules, a kick in which the ball spins around its axis. Also a **torp** or **torpie**.

toss An act of masturbation, also to **toss off**. **Not give a toss** is to not care at all.

toss it in To give up on something.

tossle The penis.

tosspot A drunkard.

toss-up An even chance of success.

toss your hat in To make a preliminary assessment.

total To wreck a vehicle in a crash or to ruin anything.

tote The totalisator.

totty A young, attractive woman.

tottymungous An extremely attractive woman.

touch 1. To borrow money from someone. 2. A person from whom money can easily be borrowed. Also an **easy touch** or **soft touch**.

touchie A touch football referee.

tough as old nails A very tough person or thing.

tough shit Tough luck. Also **tough titties** or just **tough**.

touse A euphemism for shithouse or toilet.

tout 1. A racecourse tipster. 2. Someone who watches and times racehorses during training sessions in order to gain information for providing tips. 3. A spy or informer.

town bike A derogatory term for a promiscuous woman who has sex with many different men in her area.

toy boy The young male partner of an older woman or homosexual male.

toy town 1. Any neat and new housing development. 2. Derogatory term for the ACT local government and parliament.

track The open road. Also the **wallaby track**.

the **Track** The Stuart Highway between Darwin and Alice Springs.

trackie or **trackies** A tracksuit with **trackie pants** and **trackie top. Trackie dacks** are tracksuit pants.

tracks Scars on the arms or legs caused by constant use of hypodermic needles.

trade Among homosexuals, a pick-up for casual sex.

Tradies A tradesmen's club.

train smash 1. A dish hastily made from such ingredients as eggs, sausages, tomatoes, onions, tomato sauce, beans and the like. 2. Tomato sauce.

train surfing Riding on top of a moving train carriage.

trammie A conductor or driver of a tram.

trannie 1. Abbreviation for transistor radio. 2. A transsexual. 3. A transvestite. 4. A transformer. 5. A transparency.

trap 1. The mouth. 2. A colonial police officer or trooper.

the **traps** A place in the local area that you frequently visit. It originally referred to a route along which a person had laid traps which they then had to visit regularly to check for game that had been caught.

trash 1. People viewed as worthless or inferior. Also **white trash**. 2. Verbal abuse designed to upset the opposition. Also **sledging** or **trash talk**. 3. To speak unfavourably of someone. 4. To wreck or destroy. 5. To mess up a room as a prank.

trash bag A contemptible girl or young woman considered trashy.

trashed Very drunk or stoned on drugs.

traveller A can or bottle of beer consumed while driving.

trawl To search for a sexual partner.

treadly A bicycle. Also a **deadly treadly**. From 'treadle', a lever pushed repeatedly by the foot to provide drive for a machine.

tree hugger Disparaging term for an environmentalist.

Trekkie A fan of the TV series Star Trek. Also a **Trekker**.

trendoid A trendy person.

trey bits 1. Rhyming slang for the shits. 2. Rhyming slang for tits.

triantelope A huntsman spider.

triantiwontigongolope A mythical insect or beastie that is sometimes portrayed as a bunyip-like creature in order to frighten children or naïve city-folk visiting the bush.

trick 1. The customer of a prostitute. 2. Superb or classy.

trike 1. A child's tricycle. 2. A railway fettler's hand-operated flatcar.

trip 1. Something that amazes. 2. A period under the influence of LSD or similar.

triss An effeminate male homosexual.

trissy 1. Frilly and girly. 2. In the manner of an effeminate homosexual male.

troll 1. To seek a casual sex partner. 2. Derogatory term for a promiscuous woman.

trolleyed To appear nonsensical due to drug use. Also **off your trolley**.

troopie A Toyota Landcruiser troop carrier four-wheel-drive.

troppo Crazy or insane, e.g. 'He's gone a bit troppo'.

the **trots** 1. Diarrhoea. 2. Harness racing.

trouble and strife Rhyming slang for wife.

trough lolly A urinal disinfectant lozenge.

truckie A truck driver.

true blue Dinky-di Australian, fair dinkum, proud and true.

true dinks Fair dinkum.

Trumpy A Triumph motorcycle.

trundler In cricket, a bowler who ambles in to bowl a slow–medium pace delivery.

try-hard 1. Someone who tries but fails to gain social acceptance. 2. Someone who attempts to be like someone else.

T-shirts In a game of pool this refers to the 'big' balls as opposed to **singlets** for the 'small' ones.

tube 1. A can or bottle of beer. 2. The barrel of a breaking wave. 3. The television.

tubs The drums.

tucker Food.

tucker bag A swagman's food bag.

tucker box A box for carrying food supplies. A famous monument near the NSW town of Gundagai depicts a tucker box with a dog sitting on top.

tucker fucker 1. A microwave oven. 2. A bad cook. 3. Tomato sauce.

tucker out To tire or become weary.

tug Of a male, to masturbate.

tummy banana The penis.

tune To gain sexual favours.

tune-up A beating, e.g. 'I copped a tune-up for hitting my sister'.

turd 1. A piece of excrement. 2. A despicable person.

turd burglar A male homosexual.

turd strangler A plumber.

turf 1. Territory belonging to a street gang. 2. The horseracing industry.

turkey 1. A foolish person. 2. Something that is unsuccessful.

turkey's nest A small watering hole for stock.

turn 1. A party. 2. A fuss or commotion.

turn dog To turn traitor or be a coward. Also **turning dingo**.

turn it on 1. To start a fight or argument. 2. To put all your effort into something. 3. To engage in sexual activity without restraint. 4. To provide a big feast for a party.

turn it up Stop it, cut the crap.

turn off To disgust.

turn on To arouse or excite, particularly sexually.

turn on the waterworks To begin to cry and often in a bid to gain sympathy.

turn-up When something bobs up unexpectedly, or a surprise. Also a **turn-up for the books**.

turps 1. Mineral turpentine. 2. Alcohol, e.g. 'Let's get on the turps'.

Turramurra tractor Sydney slang for city-only four-wheel-drive.

twat 1. The vagina. 2. A silly or stupid person.

tweaker A finger-spinner in cricket.

tweeds Trousers.

tweenie A beer bought between shouts.

twenty to the dozen Doing something very quickly.

twerp or **twirp** A stupid or insignificant person.

twig To suddenly realise or cotton on to something is to twig.

twinkle To urinate.

twisty A small twist-top bottle of beer.

twit A fool or silly person.

two bob Formerly two shillings now 20 cents. To have **two bob each way** is to hedge your bets. If you're **not the full two bob** you are a not very intelligent. Something that is **not worth two bob** is of little worth. To have your **two bob's worth** is to participate.

two-bob lair A man who dresses in cheap, gaudy clothes to draw attention to himself.

two-bob watch A cheap watch that doesn't work very well. Often used in phrases to indicate that someone or something is dysfunctional, like **silly as a two-bob watch, mad as a two-bob watch, bent as a two-bob watch** or it **goes like a two-bob watch**. If someone is putting on a turn they are **carrying on like a two-bob watch**.

two-dog night A cold night in the bush when you need two dogs to keep warm.

two-fifths of five-eighths of fuck-all A very small amount.

two-pot screamer Anyone who gets drunk after only two glasses, or a small amount, of beer or alcohol.

twosies A childish term for defecation.

two-up A classic Aussie gambling game where two coins are tossed in the air with bets placed on how they will fall. Also **swy** or the **national game**.

tyke 1. A Roman Catholic. 2. A small child.

tyre kicker Someone who inspects cars for sale but has no intention of purchasing one.

U

uber A prefix added to many words by young people as an intensifier. If someone is **uber-cool** they are cooler than cool. A gorgeous spunk is an **uber-babe** or an **uber-hunk.**

uey or **u-ee** A U-turn, e.g. 'Why don't you do a uey at the next corner?'To make a U-turn is to **chuck a uey** or **hang a uey**.

uggies Shortening of ugg boots, long sheepskin boots that are very popular in Australia.

ugly as a bagful of arseholes Very unattractive or really ugly Also **ugly as a hatful of spiders**. Even uglier is to be **as ugly as a bagful of arseholes tied with a string of farts**.

ugly stick A mythical stick with which someone has been hit to make them ugly.

ugly tree A mythical tree from which someone who is ugly is said to have fallen. Also **he looks like he's fallen out of the ugly tree and hit every branch on the way down**.

uh-oh, spaghetti-oh A phrase indicating that something has gone wrong or a mistake has been made.

umming and ahhing Being indecisive, e.g. 'Please stop umming and ahhing and just do it'. Also **um-ah.**

umpie Abbreviation of umpire.

umpteen An indefinitely large number, e.g. 'We sold umpteen bottles of cola today'. Also **umpteenth**.

Uncle Bob Everything is okay. From the phrase **Bob's your uncle**.

Uncle Willy Rhyming slang for silly.

unco Clumsy or awkward. Short for uncoordinated.

uncool Unfashionable, lacking in cool.

underdaks Underpants. Also **underchunders** or **underdungers**.

underground mutton Rabbit meat.

undies Short for underpants.

unfuckable Said of someone considered too ugly for sexual intercourse.

unhip Daggy or uncool.

unhung A despicable or contemptible person.

uni Short for university.

unleaded Low alcohol beer, as opposed to **super**.

unreal Excellent or wonderful, e.g. 'The dinner was unreal'.

up 1. In children's games, the person who must catch the other players. 2. A male engaged in sexual intercourse. 3. Annoyed with someone, e.g. 'She was up him for being late home'. 4. Crawling, as in **up one another**. 5. Conceited as in **up yourself**.

up and under Rhyming slang for chunder.

up a gumtree Someone who is in a hopeless position or in strife.

upper A stimulant drug.

upter No good or broken down. Short for **up to putty** or **up to shit**.

up the creek In trouble or in a predicament. You are in even more trouble if you are **up the creek without a paddle** and even worse is **up shit creek without a paddle in a barbed wire canoe**.

up the duff Pregnant.

up the pole Facing difficulties or in strife.

up there Cazaly A call of encouragement, particularly at an Aussie Rules match. Named after AFL legend Roy Cazaly.

up the spout 1. Pregnant. 2. Ruined or lost. 3. Pawned.

up the stick Pregnant.

up the track To travel north from Alice Springs to Darwin.

up to putty No good or worthless.

up to shit No good, ruined or worthless.

up you Damn you. Also **upya** and in the plural **upyas**.

up your arse To hell with it or stuff you. Short for **shove it up your arse** but often shortened to **up yours**. Also **up your nose with a rubber hose**.

up yourself Said of someone who is conceited or snobbish.

urger A racecourse tipster.

us Pronoun used by many Aussies to mean me, e.g. 'Give us a look at it'.

use To take drugs, e.g. 'He's been using for ages'.

useful as ... Completely useless. This is used is many phrases, including those with a rural theme such as **useful as tits on a bull**, **useful as a bucket under a bull**, **useful as a dry thunderstorm**, **useful as a dead dingo's donger**, **useful as a sore arse to a boundary rider**, **useful as a wether at a ram sale** and **useful as two knobs of billy-goat poop**. There are those with an anatomical theme like **useful as a witch's tit**, **useful as a wart on the hip**, **useful as a c... full of cold water** and

useful as a third armpit. Others mention things that do not go together like **useful as a glass door on a dunny**, **useful as a pocket on a singlet**, **useful as a roo-bar on a skateboard**, **useful as a submarine with screen doors**, **useful as an arsehole on a broom**, **useful as a glass eye at a keyhole**, **useful as a letterbox on a tombstone** and **useful as an ashtray on a motorbike**. Other examples include **useful as a nun at a buck's night**, **useful as a pork chop at a Jewish barbecue**, **useful as a spare dick at a wedding** and **useful as a tart at a christening**.

user 1. A drug addict. 2. A person who exploits other people in interpersonal relationships without caring about the emotional damage caused.

ute Short for utility, the great Aussie work and recreational vehicle. Also a **tilly**.

uterus A silly term for a utility vehicle or a ute.

V

vadge The vagina. Also **vag**.

vag Vagrancy. To be **on the vag** is to be charged with vagrancy.

the **Valley** The Brisbane suburb of Fortitude Valley.

vanished like a fart in a fan factory To disappear.

vasso 1. Vaseline petroleum jelly. 2. A vasectomy.

Vatican roulette The rhythm method of contraception.

VB Victoria Bitter beer. Also **veeb** or **veebers**, **Victor Bravo** and **vitamin B**, and also known by the derogatory terms **Very Bad beer, Violent Beer** and **Vomit Bomb**.

VB shoulder A sore shoulder from carrying cases, or slabs, of VB beer.

Vee Dub A Volkswagen vehicle.

veg To relax and switch off mentally. Short for vegetate. Also **veg out** or **veging out**.

vegaquarian A vegetarian who still eats seafood.

Vegas A shortening of **Bris-Vegas**, a colloquial name for Brisbane.

Vegemite An Australian product made from yeast extract and which is spread on bread or toast. It is used in the phrase **happy little Vegemite** to refer to someone who is in a good mood. **Little Vegemite** is also used of children.

Vegemite valley A derogatory term for an area where lots of dark-skinned people live.

vegie 1. Vegetable. Also **vegies**. 2. The lowest academic standard of a school subject, e.g. 'Little Johnny's only doing vegie maths'.

veranda bum A large backside.

veranda over the toyshop A polite way of referring to a man's protruding stomach.

verbal diarrhoea Someone who talks nonsense or talks too much is said to have this.

verse A child's way of saying 'play against' or versus, e.g. 'We verse them tomorrow'.

vertically challenged Someone who is short.

vet 1. A veterinary surgeon. 2. A veteran of war service. 3. To examine something.

Vic-wit A NSW derogatory term for a Victorian driver.

vid A video.

Vietnamatta The Sydney suburb of Cabramatta, where many Vietnamese people reside.

vinegar stroke The final effort of a male at the point of masturbation.

Vinnies An opportunity shop operated by the St Vincent de Paul Society.

vino Wine.

vino collapso A cask of wine.

vinyl An old-fashioned music record or album.

the **Violet Crumbles** A nickname for the Sydney Kings basketball team, whose purple and gold colours resemble the wrapping of a Violet Crumble chocolate bar.

the **virus** The HIV virus.

visually challenged An ugly person.

vitamin E The drug ecstasy.

voice like a ... Someone with an unpleasant voice can be described as having a **voice like a chain being dragged through gravel**, **a voice like a chainsaw hitting granite**, **a voice like a strangled fowl**, **a voice like a billygoat sitting on tin** or a **voice like a knife that has been stuck in a lemon too long**.

Volksie A Volkswagen car.

VPL The edge or seam of underwear as seen through an overgarment. It stands for visible panty line.

W

wad 1. A large sum of money. 2. A stupid or annoying person. 3. To **shoot his wad** is to ejaculate.

waddy A hefty club or stick.

waffle To talk nonsense or rave on.

wag 1. To deliberately miss school without a reason, to be truant. Also **wagging**. 2. An amusing person, e.g. 'That bloke's a real wag'.

wagga rug A rough blanket made of wheat bags. Also a **wagga blanket** or just a **wagga**.

walkabout 1. Something or someone that can't easily be found or has gone missing has **gone walkabout**. 2. A journey taken on foot by an Aboriginal. 3. A short walk or inspection.

walkover Something that is achieved very easily, or a heavy defeat in sport.

walk-up start 1. Anyone who is easily conned. 2. Someone believed to be very capable of carrying out a task or doing well at sport.

Wallaby Bob's cousin Rooted, stuffed or ruined. Wallaby Bob's cousin is Roo Ted. Also **Wallaby Bobbed**.

wallaby jack A sturdy vehicle jack commonly used on four-wheel-drives. It has a long handle which looks like a wallaby's tail when in use.

wallaby track The open road as once used by swagmen. Also simply **the wallaby**. To be **on the wallaby** is living as a swagman looking for work.

wallie A wallet.

wallop 1. A large quantity. 2. To punch or strike someone. 3. Strength. 4. Booze.

walloper A police officer, as seen by those on the receiving end.

wally A foolish or silly person.

Walter Mitty A person who poses as a returned war veteran.

waltzing matilda Wandering the countryside as a tramp or as a swagman looking for work.

wandering hands The hands of a man who can't keep them to himself.

wang To hit, e.g. 'I just wanged him on the head'.

wangle To get yourself out of something awkward.

wank 1. To masturbate. 2. Self-indulgence or a load of crap, e.g. 'What's he doing with a car like that? What a wank'.

wankasaurus An egotistical or obnoxious person.

wanker 1. A disparaging term for a stupid person with an overinflated opinion of themselves. Also commonly used to describe someone you don't like. 2. A masturbator.

wanker tank A city-only four-wheel-drive.

wankery Wanky behaviour. Also **wankerism**.

wankfest A group of wankers getting together.

wank off 1. To masturbate. 2. Go away.

wank on To talk at length, especially with self-indulgence.

wanky Pretentious or self-indulgent.

wanna Want to, e.g. 'Do you wanna go to the pub?'

warby Shabby, unkempt or unappealing. A **warb** is a grotty person or a derelict.

war paint Women's cosmetics.

warp speed A very fast speed.

warrigal 1. A dingo. 2. An Aborigine living in the traditional nomadic manner. 3. A wild horse.

Warwicks Short for Warwick Farm, rhyming slang for arm.

washboard stomach A stomach with well-toned, rippling muscles.

washer-upperer A child's term for the one who washes the dishes.

waste To murder or kill.

waste of space A useless person.

water burner A bad cook.

watering hole The pub or a bar.

water the horse Of a male, to urinate.

waterworks 1. The bladder and urinary system. 2. To cry. If you **turn on the waterworks** it is usually a self-induced fit of crying in order to elicit sympathy.

wax Kids' slang for partnering someone in a game or activity.

waxhead A derogatory term for a surfie in reference to the wax used on surfboards.

wedding tackle The male genitalia.

wedge A beer bought between shouts or rounds of drinking.

wedgie 1. A prank where someone's pants are pulled up sharply to wedge the clothing into the anal cleft. 2. A wedge-tailed eagle.

wee Urine or the act of urination.

weed 1. Marijuana. Also the **evil weed**. 2. A weak, puny person. 3. A surfer. 4. Tobacco.

wee juggler A Major Mitchell cockatoo. From the Aboriginal Wiradjuri word *wijugula*.

weener The penis, especially a small one.

weero In WA, the cockatiel. From the Aboriginal Nyungar language.

wee wees A child's term for urinating.

weirdo Someone who behaves in a strange or eccentric manner.

weirdometer A mythical machine that measures weirdness.

well-endowed 1. Of a man, with large genitalia. Also **well hung**. 2. Of a woman, with large breasts. Also **well stacked**.

wellies Abbreviation of Wellington boots or gumboots.

wellington Sexual intercourse. Short for Wellington boot, rhyming slang for root.

well-oiled Drunk.

were you born in a tent? A rhetorical question used to inform a person that they have forgotten to close a door.

Werribee trout Melbourne slang for a floating piece of human excrement.

Werris Creek 1. Rhyming slang for a leak, or the act of urination. 2. Rhyming slang for Greek.

westie A derogatory term for a person of low socio-economic background. It was originally used to describe someone from Sydney's western suburbs.

wet fart A fart in which some excrement also comes out.

wet sock An insipid person.

wettie A wetsuit.

whack 1. To place in a slap-dash manner, e.g. 'Just whack it down over there'. 2. To attempt something, e.g. 'I'll give it a whack'. 3. A portion or a share. 4. Male masturbation.

whacked 1. Exhausted. 2. High on drugs.

whacker A stupid person or a nerd.

whacko 1. An expression of happiness, delight or enthusiasm. Also **whacko-the-diddle-oh**, **whacko the chook** and **whacko the did**. 2. Eccentric or crazy.

whack off Of a male, to masturbate.

whack off with To steal.

whack the illy To perform a confidence trick.

whack up To share out or divide.

whacky baccy Marijuana.

whale A big-time gambler. Opposite to a **minnow**.

whale into To beat up or assault.

wham bam thank you ma'am An act of sexual intercourse, especially when it is quick and unromantic.

whammy A spell or curse directed at a person. A **double whammy** is amazing bad luck and even worse is the **triple whammy** and **quadruple whammy**.

whanger The penis. Also a **whang**.

wharfie A dock worker.

what can I do you for? A jocular Aussie way of asking 'What can I do for you?'

what do you do for a crust? How do you earn a living?

what price? What do you think of ... ? e.g. 'What price the old lady now?' This is generally a rhetorical question.

whatsit Usually used to refer to an item the name of which you can't recall. Also a **whosie-whatsit**.

what's that got to do with the price of fish? What's the relevance of what you've just said? Also **what's that got to do with the price of tea in China?** or **what's that got to do with the price of potatoes?**

what's the deal? What is going on?

what's-their-face Used to describe someone whose name you can't remember. Also **what's-her-face** or **what's-his-face**.

what's your poison? What would you like to drink?

wheelie 1. Spinning your tyres and leaving some rubber on the road. 2. Driving on the back wheel of a bicycle or motorbike with the front wheel in the air.

wheels A motor vehicle.

when the crow shits Payday.

when the shit hits the fan When the trouble begins.

whiffy Smelly, especially in regard to humans.

while your arsehole points to the ground Whenever one is alive, e.g. 'I won't go and visit them, not while my arsehole points to the ground'.

whinge To complain about something in an annoying manner.

whingeing Pom An English person who is always complaining about Australia.

whinger Someone who is always complaining.

whip around An impromptu collection of money from colleagues or friends for a gift.

whippy 1. Money stashed away. 2. A hiding place for money. 3. In gambling, the pot or the kitty. 4. The finishing post in children's games.

whip the cat To cry over spilt milk or to vent frustration over something that can't be changed.

whirly-whirly A mini whirlwind that picks up dust and rubbish. Also a **whirly-wind**.

white-ant To undermine someone or gazump them.

white can 1. A can of Carlton Draught beer. 2. A can of Swan Light beer.

whitefellow A European Australian. Also spelt **whitefella** or **whitefeller**.

white leghorn A woman dressed to play lawn bowls.

white maggot A derogatory name for an Aussie Rules umpire.

white pointers Topless women sunbathers.

white rabbits Among children, a phrase used while playing to invoke immunity from being punched or hit.

whizz Amphetamines.

the **whole box and dice** Everything.

a **whole nother** Different. Created by the insertion of 'whole' in 'another'.

whole shebang Everything or the works.

whoo A cry of excitement Also **whoo-ee**.

whoopee 1. A cry of elation, like 'hooray', but commonly used with sarcasm to express the opposite. In this sense there is also **whoopee-do**. 2. To **make whoopee** is to engage in merrymaking or sexual fun.

whooshka Something happening suddenly, e.g. 'I opened the door and whooshka, the dog raced in'.

whopper 1. A big lie. 2. Something that is very big.

whosie-whatsit Usually used to refer to an item the name of which you can't recall. Also a **whatsit**.

who's robbing this coach? A rhetorical question meaning 'stay out of it' or 'who is in charge here?'

who's up who and who's paying the rent? A question regarding the sexual and financial relationships of a group of people.

widdle 1. Urine or urination. 2. Child's talk for little.

wide brown land Australia.

wide-on Sexual arousal in a woman.

widgie A teenage female delinquent.

widow-maker 1. A dead tree branch that is likely to snap off and kill someone. 2. A very high kick in Aussie Rules which puts the marker in danger of injury.

wife beater 1. A long, thin loaf of bread. 2. A workman's blue singlet.

wife's best friend The penis.

wife starver Someone serving time in prison for defaulting on maintenance payments.

wigged out Stoned on dope.

wigwam for a goose's bridle A fanciful, non-existent object used as an answer to an unwanted question. Also a **whim-wham** or a **wing-wong for a goose's bridle**.

wild colonial boy A bushranger or nowadays a young, spirited Aussie bloke with a disregard for authority.

wild man of Bungaree An unkempt fellow.

William the Third A piece of excrement or the act of defecation. Rhyming slang for turd. Also **Henry the Third** or **Richard the Third**.

willing Eager to fight or take on any challenge.

willy 1. A wallet. 2. Money for gambling. 3. The penis. 4. To **chuck a willy** is to throw a tantrum. Also **throw a willy**.

willy-nilly All over the place or disorderly.

wimp A weak or ineffectual person.

wimpish In the nature of a wimp or gutless. Also **wimpy**.

wimp out To give in or renege in a cowardly way.

the **Windies** The West Indian cricket team.

wine-dot An habitual drinker of wine.

wing-ding A big party.

wing nut Someone with large, protruding ears.

winkers The eyes.

wino Someone addicted to wine.

win on To successfully flirt.

wipe To reject or dismiss a person, e.g. 'That's it, I've had it. I think I'll wipe him'.

wizz 1. To urinate. 2. Amphetamine. 3. The female genitalia. Also a **wizzer**.

wobbly To **throw a wobbly** is to become angry or lose you temper. Also **chuck a wobbly**.

wobigong The odd one out or something that does not go with other things.

wodge A large lump or pile.

wof A fool. An acronym of Waste Of Flesh.

wog 1. A cold or similar minor illness caused by a germ. 2. A disparaging name for an immigrant, particularly from the Mediterranean area.

wogball Soccer.

wog boy A young adult male 'wog'. The female counterpart is the **wog girl**.

wog chariot A type of car favoured by young ethnic men.

woggify To transform with 'wog' style or 'wog' culture.

woggy Something that is stereotypically ethnic, i.e. woggy food or a woggy car.

wog mansion A large, two-storey, extravagant home that is often complete with Corinthian columns and a large fountain out the front.

wombat 1. Typical, chauvinistic Aussie bloke who `eats, roots and leaves'. 2. A person who is slow-moving or slow-witted.

wombat-headed Someone who is dull, stupid or block-headed.

womble To walk with the ambling gait of a wombat.

wongi A chat among friends.

wonky Shaky or unstable.

wood butcher A rough carpenter.

wood duck Someone who is easily fooled or gullible.

wooden spoon The honour you 'win' for coming last in a competition.

woody An erect penis.

woofer A dog.

woolly woofter Rhyming slang for poofter.

Woop Woop A fictitious location that is a long way away, in the most remote areas, e.g. 'He lives in Woop Woop'.

wooza 1. Derogatory term for a young woman. Also **wooz** or **woozie**. 2. The female genitalia.

wop 1. A racist term for an Italian. 2. To take a day off school illegally or to wag.

wopcacker A great example of something.

worker's crack Bottom cleavage showing above a pair of worker's stubbies.

work like a drover's pup To work very hard.

work your guts out To work as hard as possible.

worms Thin extrusions made by spreading Vegemite on two Vita-Weat biscuits and then squeezing them together.

worrywart A person who is always worrying.

wouldn't be dead for quids Happy to be alive.

wouldn't it Dismay or disgust. It is a shortening of **wouldn't it root you**. Also **wouldn't it rip you**, **wouldn't it rotate you** or **wouldn't it rot your socks**.

wouldn't know if his arse was on fire A phrase that describes someone who is very unaware of what is going on. Also **wouldn't know it if a tram was up him until it rang its bell** or **wouldn't know if a band was up him until he got the drum.**

wouldn't shout in a shark attack Someone who is very hesitant to buy, or shout, someone a beer.

wouldn't work in an iron lung An extremely lazy person.

wowser A straight-laced person or a prude.

wowserish Prudish. Also **wowseristic.**

wowserism Puritan behaviour.

wrapped Enthusiastic approval. Also a **wrap.**

wrap yourself around To eat, e.g. 'Wrap yourself around these sangers'.

wrinklie An elderly person.

write-off A car that has been so badly damaged in an accident that it will cost more to repair than what the car is worth.

write yourself off To do something that incapacitates you, such as drinking.

wrote the book on To be an expert at something, e.g. 'Does he know anything about cricket! He wrote the book on it'.

no **wucking furries** A more polite way of saying no fucking worries.

wuss A timid, ineffectual or scared person.

wuss bag A pathetic wuss.

wussy Feeble or cowardly.

X-out To get rid of something or erase it.

X-phile A fan of the television show *The X-Files*.

XYZ A polite way of telling someone their fly is undone. It stands for 'eXamine Your Zipper'.

Y

the Y The YMCA or YWCA.

ya You, e.g. 'I'll see ya later'.

yabber To talk or chat.

yabby A freshwater crayfish native to central and eastern Australia. Also **crawbob**, **crawchie**, **lobby** or **cray. Blackie**, **bluey** and **greenie** refer to the different stages of yabby development.

yabbying Fishing for yabbies.

yack 1. To talk or chatter, e.g. 'She had a good yack with the neighbour'. 2. To vomit.

yacker Talk or chatter, e.g. 'There was plenty of yacker going on at the party'.

yaffle To waffle on. This term is common in Tasmania.

yahoo A loud mouth, a hoon or a reckless young person.

yahoo around To act in a loutish manner.

yakka Hard work, especially of the manual type.

Yank An American person. Also **Yankee**.

Yankeeland A derisive term for the United States.

Yankee shout An outing where each person pays their own way.

yank my chain To mislead or fool, e.g. 'I think you're just yanking my chain'.

Yank tank A large American car.

yap Idle conversation.

yardie 1. A general assistant in a hotel. 2. A person who does the running around in a car yard.

yarn 1. A talk or a chat. 2. An exaggerated story or a tale.

Yarra banker An orator on their soapbox on the bank of the Yarra River in Melbourne.

the **Yartz** A Strine pronunciation of 'the arts'.

yea This much, e.g. 'She's only about yea high'.

yeah, no Despite its ambiguity this recent expression is used to show agreement, e.g. 'Yeah. No, you're right on that one'.

yeah, right Sure, but often used in a sarcastic way to express disagreement.

yee-haa 1. Used to express excitement. 2. In an ironic way, it is used to denote that one is not excited, e.g. 'I've got to do the shopping today — yee-haa'.

yello A variation of hello and often used when answering the phone.

yellow 1. Cowardly. 2. Derisive term for Asians.

yellow can A can of XXXX beer.

yellow sticker A defect notice stuck to a car window.

yike A brawl or argument.

yips 1. Nervousness that causes a golfer to miss an easy putt. 2. Nervousness affecting anyone playing sport.

yip stick A broomstick putter in golf.

YMCA dinner A meal made from leftovers. It stands for 'Yesterday's Muck Cooked Again'.

yo 1. Used to call someone's attention. 2. An expression of agreement. 3. Used to show approval or pleasure.

yobbo A hooligan or lout. Also an unsophisticated or uncultured person.

yobby As befitting a yobbo. Also **yobbish**.

yodel To vomit.

yoe A ewe.

Yogie A derogatory term for a resident of Canberra and so called because ACT number plates all start with the letter Y.

yonks A long period of time, e.g. 'I haven't seen her for yonks'.

yonnie A stone used for throwing.

you beaut Excellent or wonderful.

you can't make a silk purse out of a sow's ear It is impossible to make something ugly into something beautiful.

you don't look at the mantlepiece when you stoke the fire A male phrase to express that it doesn't necessarily matter what the face of a sexual partner looks like.

you'll do A great Aussie compliment.

you'll keep An empty threat generally made when you can't think of a clever comeback.

young-un A youngster or a child, e.g. 'I took the young-uns to the show'.

your blood is worth bottling Said of a fantastic person.

youse The plural of you, e.g. 'Youse guys should have a peek at this'. Also **yers** or **yas**.

you wish A term indicating that someone has unrealistic expectations or ideas, e.g. 'Faster than him? Yeah, you wish!'

you wouldn't read about it What bad luck.

yow 1. A cry of pain. 2. Used as a warning that the police are coming. To **keep yow** is to act as a lookout.

yowie A mythical Aboriginal beast.

yucko Disgusting or repulsive.

yummo 1. Something that tastes very nice. 2. Beautiful or gorgeous.

yummy mummy A beautiful young mother.

yum, yum, pig's bum A childish exclamation used of delicious food.

yuppie A young urban professional person. Also **yup**.

Z

zack 1. Was a sixpence but now five cents. 2. To **not have a zack** is to have no money.

zambuck A St John Ambulance officer.

zap 1. To cook something in a microwave oven. 2. To change TV channels with a remote control.

zapper A remote control for a TV, DVD player or the like.

Z-car A federal government vehicle. Named because they had number plates that began with the letter 'Z'.

zeds To **push out zeds** or **stack up zeds** is to sleep.

zhuzh To fluff up.

ziff A beard.

zilch Nothing.

zillion A very large amount. Someone with a zillion dollars is a zillionaire.

zip Nothing or zero. Also zippo. Also used in the phrase **zip, zero, nada** which means nothing at all.

zizz A short nap.

zombie 1. A dull or brainless person. 2. Marijuana.

zoned out Spaced out from taking drugs.

zonked 1. Very tired. 2. Drunk or stoned.

zonkerpede An unknown creepy-crawlie or insect.

zonks A long time, e.g. 'I haven't seen him in zonks'.

zot A pimple.

Bibliography

1991, *The Macquarie Dictionary and Thesaurus,* Herron Publications, West End, Queensland. By arrangement with The Macquarie Library, Macquarie University, Sydney.

2001, Encarta Concise English Dictionary, Bloomsbury Publishing, Pan Macmillan Australia, Sydney.

Author unknown, *Australian Slang Dictionary,* Dynamo House, Melbourne.

Ayto, J. and Simpson, J., 1982, *The Oxford Dictionary of Modern Slang*, Oxford University press, Oxford.

Blackman, J., 1990, *Australian Slang Dictionary*, Sun Books, Macmillan, South Melbourne.

Cryer, M., 2006, *The Godzone Dictionary of Favourite New Zealand Words and Phrases*, Exisle Publishing, Titirangi, Auckland.

Dixon R.M.W., Moore, Bruce, Ramson, W.S. and Thomas, Mandy, 2006, *Australian Aboriginal Words in English, Their Origin and Meaning*, 2nd edition, Oxford University Press, South Melbourne.

Green, J., Newspeak, 1984, *A Dictionary of Jargon*, Routledge & Kegan Paul, London.

Hughes, J. (ed.), 1989, *Australian Words and Their Origins*, Oxford University Press, Melbourne.

Lambert, J. (general ed), 2005, *Macquarie Australian Slang Dictionary*, The Macquarie Library, Macquarie University, Sydney.

Rees, N., 1987, *Why Do We Say*, Blandford Press, Poole.

Individual contributions

Dave Shearing

Bob Snell

Gary Radford

Dave Hackett

Allen Dwyer

The late Wilga Harris

Janice Harris

Yolanda Torrisi

Students of Kinross Wolaroi School, Orange, and teacher Bruce Paine

Also by Exisle Publishing ...

The Godzone Dictionary

Max Cryer

Visitors to New Zealand are frequently surprised — and puzzled — by words and phrases in the language that locals take for granted. Not only do New Zealanders have their own accent, but they also have a rich vocabulary that is distinctive and individual.

The Godzone Dictionary is a concise A–Z of the words and phrases that make the New Zealand language and speech patterns so different. Language expert Max Cryer examines a wide range of words and phrases, shedding light on their origins and offering helpful definitions. Slang words and expressions feature heavily, while one of the unique features of the book is the large number of Maori words that have become part of the common language in recent years. The listing also includes the popular names of New Zealand sports teams (so often confused!), while an appendix of common acronyms completes the book.

Never stuffy or academic, Max Cryer brings his expert knowledge and dry wit to a book that is sure to be a reference for many years to come.

ISBN 978 0 908988 74 7

First published 2009

Exisle Publishing Limited
'Moonrising', Narone Creek Road, Wollombi, NSW 2325, Australia
P.O. Box 60–490, Titirangi, Auckland 0642, New Zealand
www.exislepublishing.com

National Library of Australia Cataloguing-in-Publication Data:
Miller, John (John Frederick), 1960–
The lingo dictionary : favourite Australian words and phrases / John Miller.
ISBN 9781921497049 (pbk.)
Bibliography.
English language–Australia–Slang.
English language–Terms and phrases–Australia.
427.994

Designed by Box Car Graphics
Typeset in 10/13pt Times New Roman condensed, 18pt Dom Casual headings.
Printed in China through Colorcraft Limited, Hong Kong

10 9 8 7 6 5 4 3 2 1